EDUCATING
FOR
VIRTUE

EDUCATING
FOR
VIRTUE

Edited by

Joseph Baldacchino

National Humanities Institute
Washington, D.C.

"Stopping by Woods on a Snowy Evening" Copyright 1923, ©1969 by Holt, Rinehart and Winston. Copyright 1951 by Robert Frost. Reprinted from *The Poetry of Robert Frost* edited by Edward Connery Lathem, by permission of Henry Holt and Company, Inc.

Library of Congress Cataloging-in-Publication Data

Educating for virtue.

    Includes bibliographies and index.
    Contents: The humanities and moral reality/Claes G. Ryn – The ethical purpose of literary studies/Russell Kirk – Education and the American political tradition/Paul Gottfried – [etc.].
    1. Education – United States – Aims and objectives – Congresses. 2. Humanities – Study and teaching – United States – Congresses. 3. Ethics – United States – Congresses. 4. Social values – Congresses.
I. Baldacchino, Joseph.
LA217.E365 1988   370.11'0973   87-63339
ISBN 0-932783-02-3

Printed in the United States of America

The National Humanities Institute is a tax-exempt organization that promotes significant research, publication and teaching in the humanities, including the social sciences properly conceived. It seeks to contribute to the reinvigoration and development of the principles upon which Western civilization is based.

NATIONAL HUMANITIES INSTITUTE
214 Massachusetts Avenue, N.E.
Suite 470
Washington, D.C. 20002
(202) 544-3158

CONTENTS

7

FOREWORD

GROWING AWARENESS of a long-term decline in academic proficiency among American students and a concomitant spread of social, cultural, and moral disorder, combined with a sense that these trends are intimately related, has given rise in recent years to a much-publicized reexamination of this country's educational policies. Such attention to the mission of our schools and teachers is much-needed, certainly, and out of it have emerged several positive developments, notably the decision of Secretary of Education William J. Bennett soon after his confirmation to encourage consideration of what he called the "three C's": Content, Character, and Choice. In selecting these categories, Secretary Bennett sought to sharpen the widely diffused discussion about the perceived weakness of American education by focusing attention on the deeper and more philosophical questions about the nature and purpose of education in Western society.

But while Secretary Bennett and kindred spirits have tried to move the debate toward fundamentals, such efforts have met with resistance from groups whose overriding interests apparently lie elsewhere. In place of qualitative and substantive issues, these groups – which enjoy great influence in the academy, the foundations, and the dominant news media – prefer to confine the discussion to the level of process, procedure, and quantity, while granting to the great "whys" and "wherefores" of education the shortest shrift. A good example of this tendency is a report issued in 1986 by a major policy organization with intimate ties to the reigning educational establishment. The report's central recommendation, since acted upon, was for the establishment of a national board to set standards for the professional certification of teachers.

Perhaps the most distressing aspect of this report, other than the almost casual way it casts aside America's two hundred-year tradition of federalism, is that, despite lavish verbal tribute to the need for higher educational standards, it says virtually nothing about the concrete shape those standards should take or the criteria upon which they should be based. Instead, nearly exclusive attention is devoted to quantitative and procedural matters, such as proposals for raising teachers' salaries, giving teachers greater control of school administration, and relieving them of routine chores through heavier reliance on technology and paid aides or assistants.

The present volume emerges from a conference, "Content and Character in Our Schools: The Renewal of American Education," which was held on January 16-18, 1987, at The Catholic University of America in Washington, D.C. The conference was sponsored by the National Humanities Institute, with the help of a grant from the U.S. Department of Education. In contrast to reports such as the one just cited, the essays that follow have much to say, and of a very specific nature, about the purpose of education and about – what is the same object viewed from another perspective – standards.

If there is a single thread that runs through these essays, it is the recognition of a universal order that transcends the flux of human life and gives meaning to it. In the Judæo-Christian tradition of the West, the power that engenders this order is called God, but – after making due allowances for differences of terminology and conceptual clarity – it can be observed that the experience of this transcendent purpose crosses all peoples and civilizations. Insofar as men act in accordance with this order, they experience true happiness and are brought into community with others who are similarly motivated. But men are afflicted with contrary impulses that are destructive of universal order. When acted upon, these impulses bring suffering and a sense of meaninglessness and despair; the result is disintegration and conflict – within both the personality and society at large. Yet so tempting are the attractions of these impulses – to yield is effortless and the payoffs in terms of short-term pleasure and ego gratification are alluring – that they frequently prevail and must be taken into account in any realistic assessment of human affairs.

This tension within the person between competing desires – the conflict between what Plato called the One and the Many – is the ultimate reality of human experience. To apprehend this reality, and to act in the light of the transcendent purpose with appropriate reverence and restraint, is the essence of wisdom; and to help deepen and strengthen this apprehension – through philosophy, history, literature, and the arts and sciences – is the overarching purpose of any education worthy of the name.

Joseph Baldacchino
President
National Humanities Institute

THE HUMANITIES AND
MORAL REALITY

Claes G. Ryn

THERE IS TODAY much talk of the need for excellence in education. These discussions are usually hampered by confusion regarding the aim of education. By what standard is excellence to be judged, and how is the goal to be achieved? Educators need answers to these questions that are put in the form of specific curricular recommendations, but tenable proposals presuppose a philosophy of knowledge and education. The purpose here is to address that primary need and to take up some epistemological issues that are basic to the formulation of educational strategy. The thesis to be argued is that the central aim of education is to strengthen our sense of reality and that the humanities must form the core of this effort.

The humanities as academic disciplines study man as a social and cultural being. Besides such subjects as philosophy, history, literature and art, the humanities include what is often referred to as the social sciences. In all of these fields books and articles are written in abundance, but the quantity of publication cannot conceal that for a long time the humanities have been declining. The educated public shows some awareness of this condition in that it does not expect scholars to have much of importance to say about those questions of life that matter most deeply to them. It seems somehow incongruous to look in today's academic circles for a modern Socrates. Most of what is there written is

13

dry, esoteric, pedantic or trivial. For a subject to become scholarly, life must evidently be squeezed from it. No wonder that many
intellectuals escape to the cheap excitement of trendy ideology
and other fads.

If the humanities are to regain a place of honor, they must
rethink their own nature and especially their epistemological
foundations. It is necessary to move beyond the kind of abstract
and formalistic reasoning that has come to dominate the theory
of knowledge. Humanistic epistemology must broaden its scope
and, among other things, incorporate ingredients from ethics and
æsthetics. Any systematic reconsideration of the purpose of education inevitably becomes a rethinking of the theory of knowledge. What is the heart of human knowledge, and how can man
move as closely to it as possible? To recognize the centrality of
the humanities and set priorities within them, it is necessary to
study with care the interaction of the three fundamental human
faculties – will, imagination and reason. Understanding their respective roles and their interdependence is the key to an adequate philosophy of education. Only one side of this large subject
can be dealt with here, the dependence of the knowledge of
reality on will and imagination.[1]

The epistemological issue that has to be faced may be introduced by means of an illustration. Most men have met individuals who are strangely prone to misunderstand everyday situations. These individuals somehow have difficulty grasping the
meaning of other persons' words and actions. Take, for example,
Dr. Smith who completely misunderstood what happened in the
last faculty meeting. You try to set him right: You explain that
Dr. Johnson did not have the kind of motive that Smith attrib-
utes to him, and that the chairman was actually facetious in his
comment. But to get Dr. Smith to see what really happened turns
out to be difficult. He easily presents arguments for his own
interpretation. These arguments are based on yet other misperceptions, but they are made clearly and persuasively. Dr. Smith is

anything but unintelligent. His various points confirm each other, and the details of his reasoning form a coherent whole, as if his view of what took place were incontrovertible. You are finally left exhausted and doubt the possibility of ever convincing Dr. Smith of what really happened.

Curiously enough, Dr. Smith is an intelligent person, by the criteria of intelligence tests perhaps even a genius. He is respected in his field of academic expertise. Still, his perception of reality has some kind of flaw. It would seem that certain decisively important facts do not register in his mind. He does not *see* the same as others. Why this is the case needs to be discussed at some length. It should be noted first that Dr. Smith's intelligence offers no guarantee that he will perceive the world realistically. On the contrary, it is his intelligence that lets him argue himself more and more deeply into illusion.

A person's tendency to misunderstand the motives and actions of others will of course not be confined to everyday circumstances. The same flaw can be expected to affect more comprehensive judgments, for example, the interpretation of history and society. A person with Dr. Smith's weakness may be a philosopher, historian or political scientist. Suppose he is a prolific historian. He argues his theses with great skill. His books and articles are full of footnotes. He responds to the criticisms of his colleagues by marshalling plentiful evidence. In debates he is brilliant. He goes from victory to victory. He becomes the leader of a new school. Many of his erstwhile critics are forced onto the defensive. Some come over to his side, if somewhat reluctantly. Others remain unconvinced, but in the face of his stream of arguments they can only mutter to themselves: "And yet the man is dead wrong."

It is necessary to take into account the possibility of a gap between rationality and reality. The purpose of drawing attention to this gap is not to assert that mankind is composed of two groups, those who have and those who lack a sense of reality. All human beings, even the wisest, have their flawed perceptions. But it can hardly be denied that some individuals are more prone to illusions than others. Illusions do not have to be naïve or utopian. They can be darkly cynical or pessimistic. Whatever the case, they reflect a lack of balance and proportion. What should be noted for the present is that such states of mind are fully compatible with formal intellectual brilliance. In this century alone one can point to many individuals of obvious intelligence who have spoken foolishly on some subjects. A number of Nobel Prize winners come to mind who have combined genius in some fields with naïveté in others.

How could this be possible? Should there not be some sort of connection between intelligence and the sense of reality? It is indicative of the weakness of the dominant schools of epistemology that they do not know what to make of the possible distance between rationality and insight. Many philosophers seem not even to be aware of the problem. One American philosopher who does recognize its existence is Eliseo Vivas. He has pointed to it in connection with an assessment of the work of Bertrand Russell. But even Vivas, who is in many respects a most perceptive thinker, is puzzled on this issue. He declares himself unable to explain how Russell could be at the same time a "technical philosophical genius" and a political "imbecile." "It cannot be explained," writes Vivas, "for it does not advance our understanding to be told that it happens every day: that geniuses have often been damned fools and often mischief-making fools at that." [2]

Vivas' inability to account for the coexistence of formal brilliance and a distorted view of reality suggests a glaring deficiency in the theory of knowledge and more generally in the philosophy of man. With this defect philosophy leaves the humanities poorly equipped to define the conditions for a realistic view of life. It can provide schools and universities little guidance when it comes to defining a curriculum that does not merely offer the students formal "skills" but imparts to them a sense of reality and the meaning of life. Many academics assert that questions of reality and the meaning of life are not proper subjects for study and discussion. In view of the widespread assent to this belief in educational circles, it is hardly surprising that some discerning commentators doubt the ability of Western civilization to survive.

There are many in the Western world today who criticize ideas that are clearly illusory but are given credence among the moulders of opinion in academia and journalism. Many shake their heads at socialists, for example, who hold on to economic doctrines that seem hopelessly discredited. But, because of the lack of understanding of the relationship between rationality and reality, the method of countering mistaken beliefs is often misguided or ineffective. The scope and nature of the problem are not recognized. Attempts are made to present an alternative to the disputed ideas, but the arguments turn out to have very limited power. It is as if the individuals with the dubious outlook did not really let themselves be affected.

The nature of this problem and how to deal with it was the subject of much of the work of Irving Babbitt.[3] Later the problem was seen by Eric Voegelin who refers to it as a "resistance to truth." As an example of this resistance Voegelin takes the survival of certain ideologies, among them Marxism. "The reasons why the various ideologies were wrong were sufficiently well known in the 1920s," Voegelin writes, "but no ideologist could be persuaded to change his position under the pressure of argument. Obviously, rational discourse, or the resistance to it, had existential roots far deeper than the debate conducted on the surface." [4]

It is these "existential roots" that have to be explored if the epistemology of the humanities and the teaching of them is to be deepened and renewed.

The idea to be developed here is that all real search for the truth depends on a willingness to confront reality. Are then not all human beings equally open to the truth? No, they are not, and this is the problem. That individuals differ in intelligence, as intelligence tests define the term, and that this may affect their ability to understand reality will not be discussed here. The point that needs to be stressed is that rationality, especially of the kind that is employed in the humanities, is not self-sufficient. Differently put, humanistic reason does not work in an experiential vacuum. The thesis to be substantiated may be formulated thus: For arguments to make any real difference, the individual's imagination and character must be such that new ideas are permitted entrance into that innermost sphere of the personality where our view of reality is formed. Conceptual thought rests on pre-rational, intuitive experience. Intuition in its turn is intimately related to an underlying orientation of will. If humanistic scholarship is to formulate realistic ideas, it must build upon realistic intuition, and such intuition presupposes a will that does not allow escape from uncomfortable parts of reality.

The relationship between rationality and intuition may be illustrated by returning to the brilliant historian with a flawed sense of reality. Let us assume that this scholar is also a talented novelist or poet. There is then reason to expect an affinity between the person's scholarly and artistic writing. Before going into this resemblance, it should be made clear that the two types of literary production are in one respect quite different. As a scholar, the person is not free to let his imagination roam. In his historical writings he claims that the events and relationships with which he is dealing were actually as he describes them. His intuition is tethered to a particular historical material. Artistic writing is not bound by this kind of facticity. Also, the scholar is primarily addressing the reader's intellect. He offers theses, interpretations, definitions, theories. As a poet or novelist, by contrast, he is primarily addressing the reader's imagination. He conveys intuitive images, concrete experiences. The individual absorbing this artistic work does not ask for documentation of events or for clear definitions, but asks for æsthetical coherence and concentration.

In spite of these important differences, there is a close connection between a person's scholarship and imagination. All humanistic scholarship requires an ability to intuit different events and circumstances. The humanistic researcher – the philosopher, historian, social scientist, literary historian, *et al.* – needs a powerful, sensitive imagination to discern the meaning of material under examination. Historical and other scholarship that is lacking in imagination becomes a sterile, bureaucratic gathering of "facts" that tries to prove its supreme scholarliness by an abundance of footnotes. Somebody has described history of that kind as "one damn thing after another." Humanistic research above the level of the pedestrian "fact"-collector depends to a large extent on the scholar's intuitive grasp of connections.

The artistic writer expresses his own basic vision of existence. His imagination conveys a kind of melody of life, a sense of what experience may contain. Scholars in general may not have the rich and penetrating imagination that can create poetry. It is good enough if they can absorb the visions of the great artists. Whether the scholar has a poetically developed or undeveloped intuition, it is this intuition that is available to him as a researcher. In the latter capacity, it is true, he lets his imagination be informed and limited by the sources and documents at hand, but it is his own characteristic intuition of life that gives concreteness and meaning to that material.

Suppose that an expert in French eighteenth century history decides to write a novel about the French Revolution. The intuition that he brings to the writing of the novel is the same intuition that he relies upon to write an historical work about the same period. It pervades his interpretation of human motives, his view of what is plausible human behavior, his assessment of what society is and can become. Whether his writing is poetical or historical, it is his intuitive sensibilities that decide if he will be drawn to the Revolution's professions of brotherly love and all its beautiful dreams for the future or be struck by its utopianism and its masked inhuman envy and hatred of the aristocracy. The "empirical" evidence will of course set some boundaries for his perceptions. In his historical scholarship this evidence will move into the foreground, but the amount of time he will devote to research into particular questions will be determined by his intuitive grasp of their relative importance.

If the imagination colors and in one sense even governs the work of the scholar, it should be quickly added that only a broad and penetrating intuition can create the conditions for insightful humanistic science. A superficial or distorted imagination must lead to poor research, however great is the scholar's formal intelligence or diligent his gathering of data. To this subject it will be necessary to return.

Our perception of reality has deep roots in the works of poets, novelists, composers and painters. Their ability to draw us into their way of experiencing the world is not restricted to moments of purely æsthetic contemplation. Truly creative imagination leaves permanent traces in the minds of others. It is true that in works of art the persons, circumstances and events are invented in the sense that historical reality is not claimed for them. But by means of them the artist tries to express what life is like. An individual who has absorbed the vision of a great artist no longer perceives historical reality quite as before. He is now more alert to aspects of experience to which he has been made sensitive by the work of art. He begins to see with the eyes of the artist. A person who has truly taken in the dramas of Sophocles or Shakespeare can hardly be unaffected in his view of the ethical conditions of human life. Can a person who has become acquainted with the impressionist painters experience nature just as before? A large number of æsthetical influences of varying artistic quality leave their mark on our way of perceiving life.

The sense of reality of an entire people is shaped to a great extent by the artistic symbols of the particular society.

It might be objected that most people lack interest in serious art. But even if they do, they are not without symbols that inspire and shape their imagination, including their dreams for the future. If, for one reason or another, they are cut off from higher art, they are the more affected by and dependent on more easily accessible symbols. Television is but one modern medium that pours out images and emotions that color the perception of life. Movies, simple novels, popular music and not least advertising play the same role.

Most people's imagination may be shaped by artistically mediocre or inferior works of popular culture, such as television "soap operas." Not even the creators of these works, including script writers and directors, are necessarily attracted to serious art. But they and those who influence them tend to be closer to it. Behind all the symbols made available for popular consumption lie the intuitive impulses of artists of some stature. They are the individuals who, by virtue of their power to capture the imagination, directly or indirectly set the emotional tone of society, for good or ill. Many or most of them may be long dead. Although the members of a society are perhaps unaware of it, they perceive reality, including the events and situations of their daily lives, largely through the intuitive mind-set that is the symbolic structure of their society. The masters of imagination behind this mind-set make people receptive to certain qualities of experience, less receptive to others. The strong intellectual and moral tensions within modern Western society and within particular individuals are at bottom tensions between incompatible intuitions of life.

In connection with stressing the influence of artists it should be underscored that their imagination is far from always attuned to reality. Often, and not least in our own century, the imagination has drawn society, including the humanities, into illusion. An entire civilization can succumb to intuition that obscures the real nature of the human condition. Whether civilization is captured by predominantly utopian or cynical misperceptions, the practical result is needless human suffering.

The purpose of these observations is to draw attention to reason's dependence on imagination. Scholarly-scientific thought gives conceptual form to experiential material that has already been constituted into a coherent whole by the imagination. Reason never works in an experiential vacuum. A scholar of cynical disposition intuits behind his documents and texts the deceitfulness and dark motives of men. A person of idyllic, utopian imagination views the same material through a rose-colored shimmer.[5] Rationality builds on this prelogical, that is to say, preconceptual, intuition of reality. Intuition makes possible an adequate perception of reality only to the extent that it does not push aside important elements of life. An imagination that lacks depth, balance and proportion will present for intellectual articulation a material that is already distorted, and not even intellectual brilliance can turn intuitive falsehood into conceptual truth. The weakness of a Bertrand Russell or a Karl Marx is not so much a dearth of formal intelligence as an imagination that slips past aspects of existence that are actually central to a realistic view of life.

The epistemological problem under discussion is intimately connected with the problem of will. It is necessary to take up the ethical dimension of knowledge, which may be introduced by an example.

Marxists are still common in the humanities, not least in the social sciences. Behind the ideology of Marxism lies an imagination that expresses certain basic sympathies and antipathies. These color the view of society and the world in general. Marxists sometimes make interesting, well-supported observations, but you also find among them a strong disinclination really to consider certain facts and arguments. They prefer not to dwell on experience that does not support their already formed intuitions and corresponding ideas. As long as the Marxist is among sympathizers or among people who can be easily converted he will expound his theses with confidence. Should he get into debate with a highly educated individual who has no difficulty countering his arguments, he is likely to avoid further discussion. For example, he would rather not pursue the fact that many so-called capitalists have shown genuine humaneness toward workers and been able to rise above class interest. Considerations of this kind are a threat to viewing society as wholly dominated by class conflict. The Marxist spitefully dismisses the uncomfortable arguments. His fundamental assumptions are too sacred to be subjected to searching analysis. Behind the scientific surface hides a resistance to reality.

Meaningful scientific discussion presupposes a willingness on the part of the participants to open themselves up to new ideas, in the final analysis to reassess the cherished imaginative structures that lie at the bottom of their own outlook. Here the ethical dimension of the search for truth comes into view. Real openness is possible only in human beings who have sufficient character to give a hearing to unwelcome points of view. Even in the scholar who is not wedded to some rigid ideology there is an inclination to resist or play down arguments and facts that may undermine deeply ingrained beliefs. We don't *want* to change. Thus, the truth is always threatened by an all too human *ethical* weakness. To bring up the question of character in a discussion of epistemology may seem far-fetched. But it can hardly be denied that truthfulness is threatened by the temptation to exclude from real consideration anything that might create dissonance within our accustomed ways of thought and imagination.

Most scholars have considerable intellectual investments to protect. Their reputations depend on their published theses' withstanding criticism. They do not want to be exposed as ignorant or less than perspicacious. But scholars are repeatedly confronted by facts and arguments that question their theories and interpretations. How are they to react? By truly weighing the validity of these intellectual challenges, or by running for cover to defend positions already taken?

Consider an historian famous for his trailblazing interpretation of certain events. In his continuing research he discovers previously unknown but very important documents that place his area of expertise in a new light and refute the earlier work that made him into a celebrated scholar. Nobody else knows of these documents. He could burn them and thus preserve his academic reputation. What will he do? It is not difficult to see that the decision faced by the historian is not just an intellectual one but an ethical one. This example is not exactly typical of the everyday work of a scholar, but it concretizes choices of greater or lesser intellectual scope that the scholar has to make repeatedly. "Shall I go through this book in a fair and open-minded manner although it seems to question some of my most treasured assumptions?" The individual's state of character will have everything to do with the answer. We are masters of a subtle self-deception that almost hides from ourselves that we repeatedly evade or explain away facts and ideas that are not pleasing to us. All of those little acts of evasion together grow into a larger self-deception. Whole intellectual systems can have such origins.

To make these epistemological connections clearer more has to be said about the relationship between imagination and will. This is a subject about which Irving Babbitt has written with originality and authority. A central theme in his work is that will and imagination tend to develop together.

First it should be pointed out that it is the imagination that gives concreteness, immediacy and texture to our wishes. It expresses our will. Hunger and thirst, for instance, are not blind desires. In the human consciousness they are articulated in particular intuitions, for example, the intuition of how a grilled piece of meat might taste or how cool spring water would feel in our throat. In general, our will finds expression in images of intuition. Our dreams for the future, the ideals we form, are manifestations of the orientation of will that dominates our personality. A particular character predisposes the individual to a particular type of imagination. So, too, a certain type of imagination inspires a certain orientation of will.

A person of essentially hedonistic sensibilities becomes used to looking for the meaning of life in its potential for pleasure. Such a human being is less sensitive to possibilities of a different kind. The imagination of a hedonist is especially receptive to poetry and other art that is carried by a similar sense of what life may contain. Hedonistic poetic visions confirm the individual in his ways. Moments of æsthetic contemplation of a life of pleasure stir in the will a corresponding wish to act. The will is invited to realize similar values in practice. The will that proceeds to action is the same will that earlier found satisfaction in a certain type of poetic intuition.

Through this interplay of will and imagination over the years, the hedonistically oriented individual builds up a particular attitude toward life. Should this individual suddenly experience moral qualms about his self-indulgence, the imagination will help him conceal or ignore them. The sense of self-reproach becomes portrayed by the imagination as the intrusion of narrow-minded and ridiculous puritan prejudice, a silly moralism that the sophisticated person knows to rise above. Egocentrical hedonism, on the other hand, is depicted by the imagination as a higher freedom, a form of self-realization that cannot tolerate petty bourgeois notions of moral responsibility. A powerfully endowed imagination is capable of putting even diabolical desires and actions in an appealing light.

In most human beings the interplay between will and imagination does not often result in intuitions of a particularly poetic type. The imagination usually works in spurts and at the service of the practical needs of the moment. In the poetically inclined and gifted individual the intuition is more easily detached from practical pressures and can turn into something more truly poetical. It should not be overlooked, however, that even when the imagination becomes poetical, it is at the same time will. Art, too, is created by a certain personality. It expresses a view of existence, a view that is the result of innumerable acts of will in the past. Through these acts the individual has experienced many things and missed many others. His present sense of life is the consequence. Because of his accustomed quality of will and imagination, the individual does not experience the world in the same way as people of a different ethical and æsthetical orientation. In the end, he does not *want* to experience the same.

It has been argued earlier that reason builds upon the intuitive material that is presented to it by the imagination. Conceptual insight presupposes intuitive insight. It has now been suggested that the direction of intuition is intimately connected with the direction of the will. This means that if the individual is to have deep and wide-ranging imagination, his will must be such as to permit this kind of openness. In contrast to this desirable state, one may consider a personality that is consumed by some strong, self-centered desire, for example, a burning career ambition. The imagination of this individual will tend to follow suit and exhibit corresponding traits: egocentrical distortion, limited scope. As a foundation for the work of rationality, the scholar needs imagination of a very different kind, imagination receptive to the whole range of human experience. Intuitive ability of that sort assumes a character that does not enslave the person to narrow and unbending biases. An open imagination and a related critical intelligence can exist only in a personality that has learnt to control self-centered passion.

But the need for intuitive scope cannot be separated from the need for discernment. The imagination must have depth and a sense of proportion as well as breadth. Intuitive insight of the most penetrating kind distinguishes what is important from what is marginal and trivial. This is to say that genuine intuitive openness includes a sense of what life actually is and should be.

Many today, and not least within the humanities, believe that we can arbitrarily choose the goals of our lives: that there is no universal standard for human behavior. To question this view one need not accept the teaching of Plato and Aristotle without qualification or adopt the specific doctrines of Christianity or some other religion. It can be argued that there is a standard of universal good that lies beyond human theories and dogmas. This standard for how we should live exists within experience itself. Some ways of acting give the individual a sense that life has meaning and is worth living, while other ways are inherently incompatible with a deeper harmony and satisfaction. Modern existentialist literature is filled with the gnawing feeling that life is meaningless and absurd. For many writers the essence of human existence appears to be anxiety and disgust. As analyzed from a classic or Christian perspective, these views of life are not unexpected. If you act on assumptions of the kind adopted by the individuals portrayed in existentialist literature, it is not surprising that you should finally be tormented by the meaninglessness of it all. According to Christianity, you can judge by the fruits. The existentialist authors show us experiential fruits that reveal the untenability of a certain attitude to life. A very different outlook typifies individuals who are shaped by the classical and Judæo-Christian traditions. An awareness of eternal values and of the importance of a corresponding ordering of character has produced fruits of another kind: a sense of meaning and happiness even in the midst of life's imperfections, injustices and suffering. Sophocles, Dante, Shakespeare and others express an intuition of the nature and goal of human existence that cannot be separated from the underlying ethical orientation that engendered it. The related sense of what is important and unimportant is not shared by artists and others whose will has a different quality and whose intuition works accordingly.

This line of reasoning might seem similar to the notion that man can decide arbitrarily what is real and unreal. It is true that man's way of experiencing life depends on the ethical-æsthetical disposition that he adopts. However, it is not possible to remake the structure of existence so that a deeper satisfaction and a better intellectual grasp of reality can be achieved in any way whatever. If man wants to discover something other than absurdity and disgust, he must work to achieve the kind of character and imagination that will build reality into his experience.

It is not possible here to develop the idea that experience itself contains a standard for how we should live. But it is necessary to say more about the connection between intuitive illumination and ethical character. Intellectual insight presupposes an intuitive dependability that is made possible in the end by the individual's having found in his actions a kind of *ethical* truth. This ethical truth is the experiential standard of life with reference to which phenomena are judged important or unimportant, noble or ignoble. If this experiential standard is obscured, almost anything becomes acceptable in the choice of goals for action. Unrealistic assumptions about man and society are exposed only at a high cost when attempts to act according to these assumptions result in human suffering.

It sometimes happens within societies and entire cultures that escapist and utopian tendencies grow strong within leading circles. The elites shrink from the high demands of civilization, evade the burdensome responsibilities imposed by circumstance. A flight from responsibility that is ethical at root begets an imagination that puts an appealing surface on the escape. Imagination in its turn pulls reason with it. A striking example of such evasion of reality was the response of Great Britain to the armaments and actions of Adolf Hitler in the 1930's. Winston Churchill's protracted, persistent and well-supported warnings about what was happening went largely unheeded, until it was too late and the world war with all its terrible suffering had to be fought. Among those in the critical years before the outbreak of the war who gave an optimistic interpretation of events and placed faith in various utopian schemes was the philosopher Bertrand Russell.

That the imagination governs or colors our reason can be illustrated with many examples from the modern Western world. One will have to suffice. For several decades overwhelming proof has been accumulating regarding the inhumanity of the political-ideological forces that are today committed to the final destruction of Western civilization. Solzhenitsyn and many others have spread an enormous and detailed body of evidence before our eyes. But it appears that we cannot bring ourselves to face the facts. Really to do so would be to face the uncomfortable and frightening consequences, including the not very appealing truth about ourselves. It has been said about Nazi Germany that most Germans knew little or nothing about the extermination camps and other Nazi horrors. What excuses can be cited by today's Westerners? We continue to look at the accumulating evidence, but we *see* little or nothing. We do not *want* to see anything. And on the heels of the will, the imagination creates convenient avenues of escape. Reality is not as terrible as it might seem. It must not be. We eagerly seize upon palliative intuitions, and in the footsteps of imagination there arise various intellectual doctrines that give conceptual form to this intuitive escape: theories of convergence, belief in popular brotherhood across the borders, and so on. In a way we do know that the Gulag Archipelago and the psychiatric wards for dissenters do exist, that they are actually there in this very moment. But are they really? Little acts of self-deception let us glide past the facts that might force us to reconsider our ways and our outlook. We do not *want* to change.

In the end, what decides our view of reality is the quality of will that sets the ethical tone in society and our own souls.

Several examples have been used to explain the interplay of

will, imagination and reason. Some simplification has been necessary and many important issues have had to be left aside or barely mentioned, among them the crucial distinction between experience that is historical and actual and experience that is purely æsthetical.[6] The main purpose has been to explain the gap between rationality and reality that originates in flawed intuition and volition. If a person's imagination is distorted, the conceptual, intellectual elaboration of his intuitions will also point away from reality. If the present thesis has any validity, a strategy for imparting a greater sense of reality must take into account the whole person. A renaissance in education and society generally will require changes in will and imagination as well as reason.

To produce any lasting results, a critique of illusory ideas must effectively question also the state of imagination and character that has made the ideas dear to the heart. The types of intuition that are prevalent among the scholars and opinion-moulders of a certain period can be studied in their richest and most concentrated form in poetry, drama, music, painting and other art. For that reason representatives of the humanities have a central role to play. Only by exposing intuitive superficiality or distortion in works of art can real doubts be created about the corresponding ideas and the way be prepared for more realistic currents of thought. A part of the great role of the humanities is to make each generation aware of the highest possibilities of life. The representatives of the humanities are trustees of the artistic masterpieces of civilization. These individuals have the difficult but all-important task of identifying and presenting to each generation those rare works of art that have let men see deeply into the nature of their own existence. These penetrating visions have a way of deflating many of the artistic reputations of the day.

The truly great works of art convey that ethical standard within experience that has been already mentioned. All real art is of course free of didactic and moralistic intent. It is partly because it is not overly bound by convention that it is able to penetrate to the heart of human existence.

A deepened sense of reality in the Western world is ultimately dependent on an ethical reorientation. But it is important to understand that the imagination, because of its concreteness, immediacy and magnetism, has great power over the will, for good or evil. Representatives of the arts and humanities therefore potentially have great influence. They can help reconstitute the imagination of Western man and through the imagination his will. They may do so by exposing the rising generation to artistic masterpieces that can bring about a cathartic cleansing of the emotions. The social sciences, too, must be highly sensitive to the role of the imagination. Our perception of society and politics is most fundamentally an intuitive vision. Beneath the various ideologies and political theories lie intuitive habits that must be scrutinized before they can be adequately assessed or refuted.

Today's Western society sorely needs a new type of cultural criticism. It needs scholars, writers and teachers who are capable of analyzing works of culture in the context of life as a whole. Above all, it needs people who can assess the quality of these works in relation to the highest values known to mankind.

There are no signs that a revitalization of the humanities will come easy. Much of what is currently written in the humanities has an almost bureaucratic cast and bypasses the important questions of life that are æsthetically expressed in art. That art is intimately related to how we view reality and that it can decisively affect how we live goes largely unrecognized by the dominant methodologies. Ideological and politicized approaches compound the problem. Many scholars in the humanities complain about a decline in educational standards and, of course, about shrinking resources. But not even unlimited resources can breathe new life into the humanities unless they first develop a better understanding of their own nature and purpose.

One of the consequences of the theory of knowledge here

presented is to rehabilitate, at least partially, the classical tradition of liberal arts. Much is valid in the old notion that the whole person must be educated, the view that is summed up in the Greek word *paideia*. If men are to achieve a strong sense of reality, civilization must shape their entire personality – will, imagination and reason. Needless to say, the various formal and technical skills often stressed in modern schools and universities do not by themselves contribute much to a deepening of humanistic understanding. But neither is bookish humanistic learning, by itself, any guarantee of insight, which is obvious from the lack of realism in many learned men. If learning is to become wisdom, it must be closely connected with the proper ethical and æsthetical education of the person.

In the effort to recover a sense of the meaning of life, the great examples of goodness, truth and beauty in the Western heritage are indispensable. And yet it is not sufficient to imitate even the noblest achievements of the past. In each historical period, keeping the great traditions alive and relevant requires work of creative adaptation and development. Art in particular is forever discovering new ways. This is the case even though the truly great works of art can be seen as variations on a theme. The classical tradition in education and culture generally used to make possible a comparative analysis of the best that had been wrought by civilization. Over the centuries the continuing assessment and ranking of the leading alternatives yielded a general direction for the enhancement of human existence. For many today, comparisons of competing possibilities of life are restricted, because of the withering of tradition, to the preferences of the hour. And the person who has never learnt to appreciate Bach or Mozart may well imagine that the Beatles represent a musical high point. An individual who has never come to know Sophocles, Shakespeare or Goethe may think that Norman Mailer is the last word in literature.

The deterioration of the classical tradition in education has led in the humanities to splintering and extreme specialization. Today, many representatives of various disciplines seem only vaguely aware that the different branches of study grow from a common trunk and that they receive their nourishment from common roots. Rare is the humanistic researcher or teacher who deals with subjects that are felt by the students to be central to their own well-being. Few are those who can place their subjects in that larger context that is life itself and for whom the boundaries between different academic disciplines are little more than administrative conveniences. In an academic environment where bureaucratic data-collectors explore ephemeral and trivial subjects, it is not surprising that the thirst for wholeness and deeper meaning sometimes finds an outlet in irresponsible opinion and imagination. To protect reason against both fragmentation and ideological pseudo-unification and to ground it in reality, the humanities must reassess their nature and purpose. To summarize the argument here presented, the person who wishes to know reality must come to share in the character of the good man and the imagination of the great artist. To assist in this effort is the great and central task of the humanities.

1. For a more comprehensive and detailed exploration of these and related problems of epistemology, see Claes G. Ryn, *Will, Imagination and Reason* (Chicago: Regnery, 1986). The book develops at length a theory of knowledge and reality.

2. Eliseo Vivas, "A Good Guy? A Bad One?," *Modern Age* (Spring 1968), 174.

3. See, in particular, his brilliantly perceptive *Rousseau and Romanticism* (Austin, Tex.: University of Texas Press, 1977), which takes up the problem of knowledge with special emphasis on the æsthetical and ethical dimensions. One of Babbitt's arguments is that in the end we are willing to accept as real only that which is known to us in experience. Babbitt's seemingly indiscriminate condemnation of romanticism has concealed that in some respects his own position resembles elements of romanticism, including German idealism.

4. Eric Voegelin, *Anamnesis* (Notre Dame: Notre Dame University Press, 1978), 6.

5. Although either utopianism or cynicism tends to predominate in a person at particular times, these two states are only apparent opposites. They actually presuppose each other and typically exist together in some combination in the same individual. Simply put, the cynic is a disappointed utopian, the utopian a refugee from the world of cynicism.

6. The distinction between historical and non-historical experience is discussed at length in Ryn, *Will, Imagination and Reason*. See also Benedetto Croce, *Logic* (London: Macmillan, 1917) and Croce, *Philosophy of the Practical* (London: Macmillan, 1913; reprint New York: Biblo and Tannen, 1967), especially Second Section, VI. Weaknesses in the English translation occasionally obscure the philosophical meaning.

THE ETHICAL PURPOSE
OF LITERARY STUDIES

Russell Kirk

THE PURPOSE of humane letters is not amusement, or self-expression, or ideological indoctrination, or even jobs for professors of English. At many American universities and colleges, one might suspect that the liberal arts were intended simply to occupy the time of young people incapable of studying anything else: yet this unpleasant phenomenon is not the true study of humane letters, but merely one aspect of modern intellectual decadence and fragmentation.

For the end of great books is ethical: that is, to teach what it means to be fully human. Every major form of literary art has taken for its deeper themes the norms of human nature. What my old friend T. S. Eliot called "the permanent things" – the ancient standards, the norms – have been the concern of the poet ever since Job and Homer. Until recent years, critics took it for granted that literature exists to form the normative consciousness – that is, to teach human beings their rightful place in the scheme of things. Such was the endeavor of Sophocles and Aristophanes, of Thucydides and Tacitus, of Plato and Cicero, of Hesiod and Vergil, of Dante and Shakespeare, of St. Augustine and St. Thomas More.

The very phrase "humane letters" implies that great literature is meant to teach us what it is to be fully human. As Irving Babbitt observes in *Literature and the American College*, humanism – derived from the Latin *humanitas* – is an ethical discipline, intended to develop the human person. The literature of nihilism, of pornography, and of sensationalism is a recent development, arising in the eighteenth century (although reaching its height in our time) with the decay of the religious understanding of life and with the decline of the central tradition of philosophy.

The normative purpose of letters is especially powerful in English literature, which never succumbed to the egoism that came to dominate French letters late in the eighteenth century. The great figures of English literature, on either side of the Atlantic, assumed that the writer is under a moral obligation to normality: that is, to certain enduring standards of private and public conduct.

From literature, even more than from our brief and bewildering private experience of life, we learn the norms of human existence. "Scientific" truth, or what is popularly taken to be scientific truth, alters from year to year – with accelerating speed, indeed, in our day. But poetic and moral truths change little with the elapse of the centuries; and the norms of politics are fairly constant. To the permanent things in human existence, humane letters are a guide.

At the beginning of this century, Irving Babbitt, in his *Literature and the American College*, predicted the coming of a time in which the teaching of literature would consist of reading Keats and Shelley to a class of girls. Something a good deal worse than that has occurred in departments of literature at a good many institutions nowadays.

When to this internal decay of humane studies is joined the twentieth-century appetite for technological and utilitarian training, the normative content and function disappear almost wholly from the modern university. Time was when everyone assumed that the analysis of humane letters must be the essence of a university's curriculum. Even today, when a new chair is proposed at Oxford or Cambridge, the formal question is put, "To what body of literature does the proposed chair appertain?" By nature, the university and the college are centers for the careful reading and discussion of important books, well written by authors of intellectual power. This gone, university and college decline to a mere congeries of vocational or specialized courses, with no central core.

Great literature deserves study for its own sake, of course. But also the practical consequences to society of the collapse of literary norms are felt in public life, soon – and in private judgment. Once the study of politics, for example, is alienated from humane letters, it becomes difficult to apprehend the norms of order and justice and freedom. In the universities and the schools, for centuries, the close study of Cicero and of Plato and of Aristotle formed the minds of the rising generation of political leaders, at every level of the commonwealth. But in the leading departments of political science at many twentieth-century universities, Statistics is king, and the notions of behaviorism have supplanted the great traditions of political theory. Increasingly, therefore, academic political science is divorced from the wisdom of our ancestors.

I am arguing that to understand the shape of society, we must apprehend poetry, in the larger sense of that word; that to know how human beings should be governed, we must apprehend the ends and norms of the truly human person. In the long run, nothing is more urgently practical than humane letters.

It is sufficiently ironical that the Soviet Russians, despite their ardent emphasis on applied science, do a more respectable work of acquainting primary and secondary pupils with serious Russian literature than we do with English and American literature. For all their dialectical materialism, the Russian Communists still recognize some place for the imagination and for the reading that forms character.

The real end of great literature is to teach us what it is to be fully human beings. I repeat: to depict the norms of human existence, though not didactically. From the Book of Job and the tragedies of Sophocles to the criticism of Samuel Johnson and the allegories of Hawthorne, the aim of humane letters was ethical; and what great writers did was to rouse the moral imagination.

What is a great writer? John Henry Newman addressed that question in 1858:

"A great author, Gentlemen, is not one who merely has a *copia verborum*, whether in prose or verse, and can, as it were, turn on at his will any number of splendid phrases and swelling sentences; but he is one who has something to say and knows how to say it. . . . He is master of the two-fold Logos, the thought and the word, distinct, but inseparable from each other. . . . from his very earnestness it comes to pass that, whatever be the splendor of his diction or the harmony of his periods, he has with him the charm of an incommunicable simplicity. . . . He writes passionately, because he feels keenly; forcibly, because he conceives vividly; he sees too clearly to be vague; he is too serious to be otiose; he can analyze his subject, and therefore he is rich; he embraces it as a whole and in its parts, and therefore he is consistent; he has a firm hold of it, and therefore he is luminous. . . . He expresses what all feel, but all cannot say; and his sayings pass into proverbs among his people, and his phrases become household words and idioms of their daily speech, which is tessellated with the rich fragments of his language."

What I have been saying so far was said by Irving Babbitt eight decades ago, although not in the same phrases; and so far as I recall, Babbitt never quoted Cardinal Newman as authority. In recent years it has seemed as if Babbitt and his friends of the "American Humanist" or "New Humanist" movement had been overwhelmed altogether by the utilitarianism and positivism of the twentieth century. Babbitt himself told his students to make use of his ideas, if they found them worthy of circulation, but not to mention his name: that would bring on rejection.

Yet very recently there has been occurring a renewal – almost a resurrection – of Babbitt's declaration that the end of literary studies is ethical. Permit me to offer you now some evidences of this reinvigoration of the ethical understanding of great literature.

* * *

First of all, I think of the brief address of Eugène Ionesco, the creator of the theater of the absurd, on accepting the T. S. Eliot Prize of the Ingersoll Awards – I being present on that occasion. Ionesco's repudiation of realism on the stage had caused many to think of him as a moral nihilist. But the truth was otherwise. Here are some of Ionesco's sentences:

"If I have shown men to be ridiculous, ludicrous, it was in no way out of any desire for comic effect, but rather, difficult as this is during these times of universal spiritual decay, to proclaim the truth.

"It is still possible, at least, to show what man becomes, or what he may become, when he is cut off from all transcendence, when the notion of metaphysical destiny is lacking in the human heart. That is, when 'realistic' reality is substituted for the Real, the eternal. It is the *sacred* that *is* what is real . . . I have tried to portray the abyss that is the absence of faith, the absence of a spiritual life. If I have consequently at times been comic, it was with the intention to teach. The comic is only the other side of the tragic; absence is only a form of the call of the presence of Him who waits behind the door for someone to open it for Him."

Like Eliot, and like Eliot's teacher Irving Babbitt, Ionesco after all is a champion of the ethical theory of literature. He would assent, I suppose, to Ambrose Bierce's definition of realism, in *The Devil's Dictionary*: "Realism, *n*. The art of depicting nature as it is seen by toads."

Ionesco's is not a solitary voice. During the past half-dozen years, a spate of well-written books by professors of psychology and of philosophy have discussed the normative function of humane letters, pointing out that intellectual virtue is formed in large part by the stories we hear or read – in childhood particularly, but lifelong too. I commend particularly the chapter "Storytelling and Virtue" in *The Emperor's New Clothes* (1985), by the psychologist William Kirk Kilpatrick. The decay of story-telling in recent attempts at moral education has worked much mischief, Dr. Kilpatrick writes.

"In a real sense the heroes of *The Iliad* and *The Odyssey* were the moral tutors of the Greeks," Kilpatrick reminds us. "Likewise, Aeneas was the model of heroic piety on which young Romans were nurtured. Icelandic and Irish children were suckled on sagas. And the Christian world, which reaped the inheritance of both classical and heroic societies, carried on this tradition of moral education with Bible stories, stories from the lives of saints, and stories of chivalry. To be educated properly was to know of Achilles and Odysseus, Hector and Aeneas, and later to know of Beowulf and Arthur and Percival and the Christian story of salvation."

The typical teachers-college educationist has forgotten or renounced this ethical purpose of literary studies. But men and women concerned for virtue in our time persist in reminding the nation of this essential function of literature. Dr. Kilpatrick touches upon the theme again in his book *Psychological Seduction*; and Alisdair MacIntyre examines it energetically in his widely-reviewed book *After Virtue: A Study in Moral Theory* (1981). Gilbert C. Meilaender examines works of literature as sources of moral understanding in his volume *The Theory and Practice of Virtue* (1984). And I commend to you particularly the treatment of the moral imagination in Craig Dykstra's book *Vision and Character: A Christian Educator's Alternative to Kohlberg* (1981).

Mr. Dykstra analyzes perceptively and at some length my friend Flannery O'Connor's story "Revelation." That is an admirable example in recent years of fiction's power to open the eyes and wake the conscience.

Ruby Turpin, captive to an evil imagination of the heart, fancies herself saved. Then an angry child hits her in the head with a book, and Mrs. Turpin perceives a new image of herself: "an old wart hog. From hell." This is a revelation, and through an image, not through an abstract message in words. Thus, indeed, humane literature works upon the moral imagination: not through preaching, but rather through summoning up images of good and evil from the numinous depths of the soul. The tremendous reputation attained posthumously by Flannery O'Connor, a shy Georgia girl and a great master of moral and mystical fiction, is evidence of the growing critical and popular interest in the ethical power of imaginative writing.

Such recognition of the educational power of humane letters now may be found in the United States Department of Education. What a change from the sociological doctrines of literature prevalent in the Office of Education a few years ago! Consider, for instance, a talk by Dr. William Bennett, Secretary of Education, entitled "Moral Literacy and the Formation of Character," delivered in New York City on October 30, 1986. Mr. Bennett is sufficiently bold to recommend that young people learn about traits of character by acquaintance with the literature of the Bible; he mentions "Ruth's loyalty to Naomi, Joseph's forgiveness of his brothers, Jonathan's friendship with David, the Good Samaritan's kindness toward a stranger, Cain's treatment of his brother Abel, David's cleverness and courage in facing Goliath." What gall and wormwood to the American Civil Liberties Union! He points out that those Biblical stories "shouldn't be thrown out just because they are in the Bible. As Harvard psychiatrist Robert Coles recently asked, 'Are students really better off with the theories of psychologists than with the hard thoughts of Jeremiah and Jesus?' Knowing these hard thoughts is surely part of moral literacy and it does not violate our Constitution."

Consider, moreover, an article in the pages of *Policy Review* by Dr. Gary Bauer, Under Secretary of Education. Its title is "The Moral of the Story: How to Teach Values in the Nation's Classrooms." Mr. Bauer's literary examples are diverse: Aesop's Fables, the collections of the Brothers Grimm, Hans Christian Andersen's fairy tales, Dostoyevsky's *Crime and Punishment*, Kipling's *Jungle Book*, *Pinnochio*, Harper Lee's *To Kill a Mockingbird*, *Hamlet*, *Lear*, Homer, the Arthurian legends, Flannery O'Connor. "Perhaps the method of moral education that would harmonize best with the existing curriculum," Dr. Bauer writes, "would be to demonstrate the working out of moral rules through experience. . . . Sometimes conflict in the areas of history or literature provides a wonderful dramatization of moral ideals set against each other. . . . I have great confidence in the power of stories to teach. Flannery O'Connor once said that 'A story is a way to say something that can't be said any other way–you tell a story because a statement would be inadequate.' The literary device of showing instead of telling is a very effective way to convey truths to young minds."

Amen to that. The Humanist Manifesto of John Dewey and his set no longer is Holy Writ in the national educational apparatus, one gathers; and the dogmatic educational utilitarianism that the National Education Association and its allies began to clamp upon American public instruction so early as 1913 – why, that domination is shaken. Once more, among scholars and educational administrators, the ethical power of humane letters rears its classical features.

*   *   *

Will teachers of literature, in these closing years of the twentieth century, agree to introduce young people, at every level of schooling, to that literature which teaches us what it is to be fully human; that literature which does not deny that there exist distinctions between virtue and vice?

When I used to be director, editor, and author of a social-science textbook series, occasionally we would confer with classroom teachers. I found that any mention of "values" frightened or angered many of them. "We're not hired to be indoctrinators," some would declare. And some would deny that any true "values" existed.

Now I shared their uneasiness with that treacherous and amorphous term "values." As Dr. Peter Kreeft puts it in his most recent book, *For Heaven's Sake*, "Values are like thoughts, like ghosts, undulating blobs of psychic energy." The positivistic sociologist would reduce our moral order to personal preferences called "values." But what our age stands in need of is not these personal preferences denominated value-judgments. It is virtues that we require: the practice of moral duties and the conformity of one's life to the moral law.

So I recognize validity in teachers' objections to imparting "values." But why should they object to "indoctrinating"? The word *doctrine* means a teaching; one cannot teach without imparting doctrines. We indoctrinate when we teach the multiplication table, or when we point out that the earth is round. We indoctrinate when we teach that some books are better than other books. To contend that no judgments may be made is itself a doctrine – and a baneful one. To indoctrinate in amorphous personal preferences, "values" without foundation in reason, authority, or custom, indeed would be very wrong for a teacher. But to indoctrinate in standards about which there has been a critical consensus for a great while – perhaps for centuries – is a natural function for a teacher.

Then let us cast away this "value-preference" fad and talk realistically.

As Professor Jon Moline wrote five years ago in the pages of *The American Educator*, "If we accept uncritically the popular 'values' terminology, we are suggesting inadvertently that on questions of right or wrong or good and bad there is nothing substantial to find out, that reasoning, evidence, and argument are inappropriate, and that these are matters for arbitrary, unarguable, 'personal' decision. Moral scruples come to seem inconsequential, like a distaste for cauliflower. . . . I submit that we drop the terminology and speak boldly of right and wrong, good and evil, duties and responsibilities, not 'values.' "

That is well and truly put. Are teachers of literature in this land, most of them, now ready to confess that wrong is not right? Or, as Samuel Johnson said of the man who professed to recognize no distinction between virtue and vice, must we count our spoons when they leave?

Approaching as I am that age at which a writer may be permitted to quote from his own earlier works, I venture to offer you a relevant passage from my book *Enemies of the Permanent Things*, which first appeared in 1969 and obtained a second edition in 1984. I am touching upon the duty to preserve a continuity of mind in a culture.

In this, I wrote nineteen years ago, "the man of letters and the teacher of literature have a principal responsibility. I do not hesitate to say that theirs is a sacred function: they are keepers of the Word. It is they who, more than the statesman, remind us of what Edmund Burke calls 'the great primæval contract of eternal society, linking the lower with the higher natures, connecting the visible and invisible world, according to a fixed compact sanctioned by the inviolable oath which holds all physical and all moral natures, each in their appointed place.' It is they who guard this contract of those who are dead, and those who are living, and those who are to be born. If this contract, this law of continuity, is broken, Burke continues, 'nature is disobeyed, and the rebellious are outlawed, cast forth, and exiled, from this world of reason, and order, and peace, and virtue, and fruitful penitence, into the antagonist world of madness, discord, vice, confusion, and unavailing sorrow.'

"Just this is the punishment of our rebel generation, which has thrown away the literary heritage of the past quite as it has broken with the moral and social prescriptions of traditional civil social existence. In some measure, the guardians of our literature have been overwhelmed by the deluge of industrialism, mass schooling, and physical alteration of society. But probably it is true that no dominant class in society ever is overthrown simply by a force from below; what undoes the masters of the state is a failure of nerve, a disease of their confidence. And probably it is true, similarly, that no set or school of men who stand for an ancient cultural inheritance ever is broken simply by the blow of an innovating system of thought; when the old order of civilization reels and falls, it is because the keepers of the Word no longer are confident in their truth. I am inclined to think that humane learning has been terribly injured in our time because the people who are entrusted with the conservation of humane letters have forgotten the true meaning of humanism; and I believe that English literature has been treated with contempt in our schools and our colleges because of what a friend of mine calls 'the treason of the English teacher.' "

The teacher of literature, nevertheless, is less treacherous than the teacher of Education with a capital E. Professor Christina Hoff Sommer, who opposes the value-preferences notion of moral instruction, found herself assailed at a conference of educationists; it was demanded that she identify clear issues of right and wrong. Here is her reply:

"It is wrong to betray a friend, to mistreat a child, to humiliate someone, to torment an animal, to think only of yourself, to lie, to steal, to break promises. And on the positive side, it is right to be considerate and respectful of others, to be charitable, honest, and forthright."

Could anyone deny these affirmations? Oh, yes: some of Dr.

Sommer's colleagues did, regarding these alleged norms as mere value-preferences. I have encountered professors who found themselves unable to agree, on any "absolute" standard, that Jesus probably was a better person than Nero. The word "professor" originally signified a person who strongly affirmed certain truths of reason. If one believes in no truths, why profess to be a professor? Why not go into some more lucrative line of work? Or may it be that the professorial nihilist would fail at any other line of work?

Let me conclude by mentioning one more book concerned with the ethical purpose of literature: Susan Resnick Parr's *The Moral of the Story: Literature, Values, and American Education* (1982). (Couldn't she have written *norms* rather than *values*?) Dr. Jon Moline, reviewing the book, summarizes Mrs. Parr's preface and first chapter, which point out the prevalent problems and attitudes of students: "students' widespread moral apathy, lack of reflectiveness, lack of perspective on their own past or on their continuity with previous generations, poor analytic skills, cynical or naïve misconceptions about human motivation, blindness to story elements caused by an inability to conceptualize, lack of realism about personal efficacy and power, fatalism, passivity, vulnerability to promises of easy solutions, egoism, and tendency to isolate from experience what they know and what they believe to be right and wrong."

Just so. Do not all of us know the students of whom Dr. Parr writes? Students, or pseudo-students, who have learnt nothing of normality, in their study of literature or history or any other discipline? Students whose habitual cheating is their only reliable habit in the Ivory Tower? More than in Irving Babbitt's day, the consequences of this nihilism are now obvious enough in our society. Even those professors who deny the existence of moral standards may have occasion to reflect after being mugged by a young person whose value-preference it is to look out for the prosperity of Number One; or after being operated upon by a surgeon whose custom it is to accept as many patients as possible, despite his lack of competence in certain branches of his science.

Dr. Parr assigns some sixteen novels and stories to students, in the hope of making them aware that they are part of the larger human community; waking them, indeed, to some degree of awareness of what full humanity comes to. I know well a dozen of her selections: *Huckleberry Finn, The Scarlet Letter, The Turn of the Screw, The Heart of Darkness, The Death of Ivan Illych, The Metamorphosis, The Stranger, The Invisible Man,* Charlotte Perkins Gilman's story "The Yellow Wallpaper," Faulkner's stories "The Barn Burning" and "Dry September," and *The Great Gatsby.* Upon a little reflection, will not anybody who has read these novels and stories begin to perceive how they might be employed as instruments of moral education, without didacticism and without taking refuge in "values clarification"?

Literature is the breath of society, transmitting to successive rising generations, century upon century, a body of ethical principles and critical standards and imaginative creations. Our literary patrimony constitutes a kind of collective intellect of humanity, the filtered wisdom of our ancestors. Our moral adversity begins to open our eyes to the true function of humane letters, in these bent years; and conceivably by the beginning of the twenty-first century the surviving readers of important books may have developed a taste for truly humane letters, very different from the corrupted prickly pears and Dead Sea fruit of literature, at the present hour so popular with major book-review media.

"The ideal of the American is external
freedom and inner control."

EDUCATION AND THE
AMERICAN POLITICAL TRADITION

Paul Gottfried

VIRTUALLY EVERYONE who ventures an opinion about education in America agrees that high among its goals is the preparation of students for citizenship. Particularly in a self-governing polity such as ours, it is crucial that the rising generations be made ready and able to participate in society in ways that will contribute most effectively to the common good. For this to happen, the educational experience must optimally be such as to awaken in the student a sense of membership in a community that transcends his own narrow interests: a community defined by its national experience and tradition. What is the nature of the specifically American experience? And what are the requisites of knowledge, imagination, and character that are most conducive to constructive participation in it? In answer to these questions, much can be learned from Irving Babbitt, the brilliant – albeit controversial – writer whom many number among the most significant American literary scholars and cultural thinkers of this century.

Babbitt's most comprehensive treatment of social-political questions, *Democracy and Leadership*,[1] appeared in 1924. The work confirmed the negative judgment his critics already held of Babbitt as an enemy of popular democracy, commerce, and humanitarian politics. Though his detractors – who in the 1920s included Sinclair Lewis and John Dewey – have affected high-

brow culture more than his followers, Babbitt's ethical and political views still resonate within certain circles. Starting with T. S.
Eliot, his students at Harvard, and continuing with Russell Kirk,
Peter Viereck, and Folke Leander at mid-century, down to more
recent writings of George Panichas, J. David Hoeveler, Jr., and
Claes G. Ryn, Babbitt has found eloquent support among tradi-
tionalist critics of American society.[2] There are self-evident connections between Babbitt's remarks on egalitarian democracy
and those of postwar American conservatives. Rereading
Democracy and Leadership for the first time in twenty years, I
was struck by the parallel between Babbitt's observations on
American government and contemporary criticism of the bureaucratic state, redistribution of earnings, and sentimental approaches to social problems.

For all these oft-noted thematic bridges, Babbitt was too much
his own man to have been merely a precursor of the contemporary Right. He despised Henry Ford and other creators of a
consumer society who he thought were inflating the popular
appetite for luxury. He mocked business magnates for their
unwarranted faith in disarmament as a means of ending interna-
tional strife. Babbitt scorned American expansionism, which he
identified largely albeit not exclusively with the new nationalism
of Theodore Roosevelt. In an observation that foreshadows the
argument of Robert A. Nisbet and other social theorists, Babbitt
maintained that America's involvement in overseas expansion
would irreversibly tilt the balance against traditional community
in favor of a growing managerial state. This expanding state
would justify itself by promoting an imperial America with global
and domestic commitments. Babbitt also contended that an appeal to property rights by big business interests would result in
cheapening the very rights invoked. The resulting identification
of property with corporate gains and stocks would enable state
managers and humanitarian reformers to argue convincingly that

all property, including the family farm, should be under state control.

Though Babbitt was critical of business interests, one should be careful about identifying him too closely, as does J. David Hoeveler, Jr., in *The New Humanism: A Critique of Modern America, 1900-1941*, with what are today called neoconservatives. Like the neoconservatives grouped around *Commentary*, *The Public Interest*, and *The American Spectator*, Babbitt, according to Hoeveler, favored a conservative welfare state. We are told that Babbitt inclined toward a regime that protected the weak against rapacious business interests and that maintained its democratic character without surrendering to popular passions. These remarks are at least partly true but must be put into context. Babbitt defended the painstakingly controlled experiment in democracy that he associated with the American constitution. Claes G. Ryn in *Democracy and the Ethical Life* carefully explicates his as well as Babbitt's views on this subject.[3] Ryn, who acknowledges his debt to Babbitt as a political thinker and æsthetician, discusses those elements of the Constitution that serve to filter and deflect the popular will. Babbitt scolded Jeffersonian Democrats and their epigones for trusting the virtues of the common man too much; he linked the mystique of democracy to an increasingly sentimental and morally undisciplined egalitarianism, leading America socially and culturally to ruin. Babbitt admired Washington and Lincoln, one for creating the federal union and the other for saving it. He depicted Washington and Lincoln as leaders with a sense of limits. Significantly, he rejected the portrayal of Lincoln as an emancipator or egalitarian rather than as the preserver of the American nation. The "federal principles" Babbitt ascribed to Washington and Lincoln provided for an exceedingly limited national government that functioned through checks and balances. Lincoln's assumption of dictatorial power during the Civil War Babbitt considered justified, but not in terms of any crusade against slavery. Lincoln suspended the Constitution for the very reason that he gave, to preserve the American nation-state as the framework of constitutional government.

Unlike many today, Babbitt viewed a bureaucratically run welfare state not as an improvement on populist or plebiscitary democracy but as a dubious departure from the original and authentic American regime. America was intended to be a country of families, communities, and vigorous local authorities, with a government that protected social institutions without trying to manipulate or replace them. Among those forces that Babbitt believed most threatened these arrangements were the ideas embodied by Woodrow Wilson. Babbitt thought of Wilson as someone who tried to make reality conform to abstraction. Whether proclaiming a "crusade for democracy" during World War I or expanding the civil service as an instrument of enlightened government, Wilson, as viewed by Babbitt, was a political utopian entrapped in private fantasies that "do not correspond to things." Babbitt noted Wilson's reputation as a university president who while in the White House received consistently high grades from college presidents.

The Wilson whom Babbitt criticized represented a tendency that he deplored in both education and government: the replacement of older standards of conduct by an ethic of public service. This ethic was basic to the educational and administrative programs that American Progressives sought to enact in the early twentieth century. John Dewey and the founders of teachers' colleges considered public service-oriented education essential for a self-improving democracy. Democratic and Republican Progressives who built federal and state bureaucracies appealed to the ideal of service as the sheet-anchor of sound government. Babbitt, by contrast, attacked this ideal as inconsistent with the political culture implicit in the Constitution. He cited the opening lines of Book Eight of Aristotle's *Politics* to underline the problematic nature of Americans' adopting a public-service educational ideal. Aristotle had taught that each form of government had its appropriate habits of mind; the founders of a city had therefore the duty to plan for a public education that taught the values associated with the regime. The better ingrained was the corresponding habit of mind, the more firmly in place was the government.

The American government of ordered liberty, Babbitt maintained, could not afford to teach an ethic of public service that really concealed the will to power. Those who glorified public service were striving to control others – while claiming allegiance to an abstract public. Administrators and educators spoke of service when they actually meant power. They used the tropes of democracy and fairness to conceal their plans for broad social reconstruction, in short, for a hidden agenda that satisfied their vanity.

True education in America – that reflected the character of the regime – would aim at teaching self-control, not self-deception about one's imperial passions. Babbitt cited a passage by his student Stuart P. Sherman that contrasts the Puritan ethic of self-restraint in the context of political liberty with the German Lutheran view of inner freedom as something compatible with political coercion. Though Babbitt recognized the distorting effect of World War I hysteria on Sherman's observation and the political coercion practiced by at least some New England Puritans, he nonetheless believed Sherman was correct about the general tendency, though not always the practice, of American Puritans. "So far as we are true children of the Puritans," Babbitt wrote, "we may accept the contrast established by Professor Stuart P. Sherman between our own point of view and that of the German: 'The ideal of the German is external control and "inner freedom"; the government looks after his conduct and he looks after his liberty. The ideal of the American is external freedom and inner control; the individual looks after his conduct and the government looks after his liberty. Thus *Verboten* in Germany is pronounced by the government and enforced by the police. In America *Verboten* is pronounced by public opinion and enforced by the individual conscience. In this light it should appear that puritanism, our national principle of concentration, is the indispensable check on democracy, our national principle of expansion. I use the word "puritanism" in the sense given to it by German and German-American critics: *the inner check upon the expansion of natural impulse.'* " [4]

It would be fair to say that Babbitt considered Puritanism not as an established church but as a habit of mind indispensable for the survival of American freedoms. He made this judgment not for æsthetic reasons (his taste in literature and literary criticism, as T. S. Eliot observed, ran strongly in a French Catholic direction). Nor did his judgment of Puritanism come from sympathy for the moral crusades of Protestant social activists in the nineteenth and twentieth centuries. Babbitt held no brief for either Abolitionists or Prohibitionists, both of whom he mocked as power-hungry and meddlesome. He defended Puritanism because its ethic of self-restraint had served to check American appetites and vices in the past. Without Puritanism, or something like it, Americans would be more likely to indulge their base passions. One of these passions, the *libido dominandi*, the demonic drive to make others objects of one's control, was precisely what at its best religion, including Puritanism, tried to turn inward by teaching self-mastery.

The American government, founded on the principle of outward liberty, could operate effectively only in the midst of a flourishing Puritan ethic. The weakening of that ethic, which Babbitt saw, for example, in the triumph of the Unitarian view of human nature over the Calvinist one in nineteenth-century New England, distressed him profoundly. He believed it imperative to warn men against their innate weakness of character – and utter folly to preach man's goodness to those who were morally complacent or lax. Never did he believe that any ethic would suffice to keep American society intact. Only a settled faith, coextensive with the history of the nation, could safeguard the ethical under-girding of our political life. Unhappily, Babbitt also suspected the faith of his fathers had been irretrievably eroded. He himself was known to be a theological skeptic who recommended religion for cultural and utilitarian reasons.

Babbitt's relationship to Christianity was the subject of censor-ious remarks and allusions in T. S. Eliot's *After Strange Gods: A Primer of Modern Heresy*. Compiled from lectures delivered at the University of Virginia in 1933, the book betokens the conver-sion to Anglo-Catholicism undergone by its author and the disavowal of Babbitt as a moral guide. Russell Kirk details this brief against Babbitt in a comprehensive introduction to the newly republished *Literature and the American College*, which one may consult for a sympathetic yet balanced restatement of Eliot's criticism.

Of this brief, only one part need concern us here, Eliot's dogged assertion that Babbitt's thinking gave evidence of "the decay of Protestantism":

His attitude towards Christianity seems to me that of a man who had no *emotional* acquaintance with any but some debased and uncultured form . . . . It would be an exaggeration to say that he wore his cosmopolitanism like a man who had lost his *complet bourgeois* and had to go about in fancy dress. But he seemed to be trying to compensate for the lack of a living tradition by a herculean, but purely intellectual and individual effort. His addiction to the philosophy of Confucius is evidence: the popularity of Confucius among other contemporaries is significant. Just as I do not see how anyone can expect really to understand Kant and Hegel without knowing the German language and without such an understanding of the German mind as can only be acquired in the society of living Germans, so *a fortiori* I do not see how anyone can understand Confucius without some knowledge of Chinese and a long frequentation of the best Chinese society . . . .

Confucius was not born into a vacuum; and a network of rites and customs, even if regarded by philosophers in a spirit of benignant skepticism, makes a world of difference. But Confucius has become the philosopher of the rebellious Protestant. And I cannot but feel in some respects Irving Babbitt, with the noblest intentions, has merely made matters worse instead of better.[5]

However, it may be an exaggeration to claim or even suggest that Babbitt abandoned Christianity, or a desiccated form thereof, to dabble in Oriental religion. He was, after all, a Sanskrit scholar who translated the Vedas: an achievement that hardly jibes with that dabbler's enthusiasm that Eliot associates with his reading of Oriental theology. Moreover, Babbitt exalted the attempt to combine Christian values and humane learning in Western education. In *Literature and the American College*, he recognizes the inherent tension between Christian faith and philosophy, and commends the efforts to achieve an educational compromise between them. Despite the occasional bad blood between religionists and philosophers, their interrelationship had produced vital intellectual and moral traditions in the West: "[T]he effort to make the ancient humanities and arts of expression tributary to Christianity was in many respects admirable, and the motto that summed it up, *sapiens atque eloquens pietas*, might still, if properly interpreted, be used to define the purpose of the college." [6] Though one might quibble about the intended meaning of "if properly interpreted," more significant is that Babbitt favored a continued role, if possible, for Christian humanistic education.

Despite Eliot's stricture, it was Babbitt, more than his disappointed student, who understood the need for a *rooted* religion as the basis of American culture and government. Unlike Eliot, a transplanted American of New England stock who opted to become an Englishman, Anglo-Catholic, and monarchist, Babbitt accepted his fate as an American within the confines of an eroded Puritan culture. He embraced his fate as the last Puritan and tried to retrieve what he could from the wreckage of the original American religious heritage, which also happened to be his own. In *Democracy and Leadership*, we learn that the "significant changes in our national temper in particular are finally due to the fact that Protestant Christianity, especially in the Puritanic form, has been giving way to humanitarianism. The point is worth making because the persons who have favored prohibition and other similar 'reforms' have been attacked as Puritans. Genuine Puritanism was, however, a religion of the inner life. Our unionist leaders, Washington, Marshall, and Lincoln, though not narrowly orthodox, were still religious in the traditional sense. The struggle between good and evil, as they saw it, was still primarily not in society, but in the individual. Their conscious dependence on a higher or divine will could not fail to be reflected in their notion of liberty." [7]

Eliot was correct in noting Babbitt's "herculean but purely intellectual effort" to "compensate for the lack of a living tradition." Nonetheless, Eliot underestimated the realism and self-honesty that informed this effort. True, Babbitt emphasized the classical foundations of good education and the parallels between Christianity and Platonism and between Western and Oriental theology, but he never lost sight of the practical dimension of expressing and acting on these views. His educational prescriptions were value-related, and they were intended to counteract humanitarian sentiments and lust for power, each a form of emotional self-indulgence incompatible with the habits of mind and character needed to preserve republican government.

Babbitt's humanism was not simply about great books or developing an inner check against emotional excess. It was an attempt to preserve republican virtue after its Puritan roots had begun to dry up. Observing that philanthropy had only limited value in improving morals, Babbitt wrote: "Our real hope of safety lies in our being able to induce our future Harrimans and Rockefellers to liberalize their own souls, in other words to get themselves rightly educated. . . . We are told that the aim of Socrates in his training of the young was not to make them efficient, but to inspire in them reverence and restraint; for to

make them efficient, said Socrates, without reverence and restraint, was simply to equip them with ampler means for harm."[8]

Babbitt quotes the vindication of Socrates in Book Four of
Xenophon's *Memorabilia* to stress the necessary link between
self-discipline and sound government. Xenophon's Socrates, as
Babbitt undoubtedly perceived, tied moderation to reverence, or
a sense of the holy, when he gave advice about educating citizens.
We know that Babbitt, too, accepted this linkage, however much
he made plans to inspire republican virtue in what he considered
religiously decayed surroundings. As he watched the descent of
American Protestantism into an abstract sympathy for one's
fellow-man (though for no fellow-creature in particular), justifi-
cations for acquisitiveness, and various utopian projects, he never doubted that his recommendations were by themselves inadequate for saving American society. Amid some observations
about cultural disintegration put into *Literature and the American
College*, Babbitt warns, "Unfortunately, this whole search of our
humanitarians for some ingenious mixture of altruistic sympathy
and 'enlightened self-interest' that will take the place of religious
restraint, is too much of an order with the search on the physical
plane for the secret of perpetual motion. In the absence of
religious restraint, not only individuals but society as a whole will
oscillate violently between opposite extremes, moving as we see
it doing at present, from an anarchical individualism to a utopian
collectivism."

Not even the later Eliot could have described with more
pathos and critical acuity the spiritual breakdown of modern
societies. Babbitt did it as a concerned American looking specifically at America, not at the wasteland as a metaphor for moder-
nity in general. Perhaps the most personally felt and certainly
most moving passage in *Literature and the American College* deals
with a cultural and visual change in New England life. Observed
Babbitt:

A few years ago I was walking one Sunday evening along a country road in a remote part of New England, and on passing a farmhouse saw through the window the members of the family around the lighted lamp, each one bending over a section of a "yellow" journal. I reflected that not many years before the Sunday reading of a family of this kind would have been the Bible. To progress from the Bible to the comic supplement would seem a progress from religious restraint to a mixture of anarchy and idiocy.[9]

This was not the past as evoked by a religiously insensitive, dryasdust intellectual. It was the kind of nostalgic memory of a virtuous past combined with jeremiads against a fallen present that one encounters in a Hebrew prophet – or, even more to the point, a Yankee preacher. Whatever else Babbitt was about – such as the meeting of East and West in the greatest moral teachers and the upholding of classical against romantic artistic and literary standards – he remained self-consciously American in his religious and political concerns. The recovery of American virtue might be aided by searching among the treasures of other civilizations, but it had to draw its sustaining power, he believed, from sources closer to home. Babbitt might have responded to Eliot that the suitable cure for American spiritual problems was predominantly a domestic one. Singing "God Save the King" would not uplift Americans who had forgotten the "Author of liberty."

1. Irving Babbitt, *Democracy and Leadership* (Indianapolis: Liberty Classics, 1979; first published in 1924).

2. See, for example, Folke Leander, *Humanism and Naturalism: A Comparative Study of Ernest Seillière, Irving Babbitt and Paul Elmer More* (Göteborg, Sweden: Elanders Boktryckeri, 1937); *Irving Babbitt: Man and Teacher*, edited by Frederick Manchester and Odell Shepard, containing thirty-nine memoirs by various writers (New York: Greenwood Press, 1969; first published in 1941); Russell Kirk, *The Conservative Mind* (Chicago: Regnery, 1953; 1986); Peter Viereck, *The Unadjusted Man: A New Hero for Americans* (Westport, Conn.: Greenwood Press, 1973); J. David Hoeveler, Jr., *The New Humanism: A Critique of Modern America, 1900-*

1940 (Charlottesville, Va.: The University of Virginia Press, 1977); George A. Panichas, "The Critical Mission of Irving Babbitt," in his collection *The Courage of Judgment* (Knoxville, Tenn.: The University of Tennessee Press, 1982); Claes G. Ryn, *Will, Imagination and Reason: Irving Babbitt and the Problem of Reality* (Chicago: Regnery Books, 1986); and *Irving Babbitt in Our Time*, edited by George A. Panichas and Claes G. Ryn, containing ten essays by various writers (Washington, D.C.: The Catholic University of America Press, 1986).

3. Claes G. Ryn, *Democracy and the Ethical Life* (Baton Rouge: Louisiana State University Press, 1978).

4. *Democracy and Leadership*, 277-78.

5. Quoted in Russell Kirk, "Introduction," *Literature and the American College: Essays in Defense of the Humanities*, by Irving Babbitt (Washington, D.C.: National Humanities Institute, 1986; first published in 1908), 57-58.

6. Babbitt, *Literature and the American College*, 80-81.

7. *Democracy and Leadership*, 277.

8. *Literature and the American College*, 108

9. *Ibid.*, 105.

THE HUMANITIES IN SECONDARY EDUCATION

Peter J. Stanlis

MY SUBJECT is the humanities in American high schools, with particular emphasis upon the role of literature. My conception of the humanities is practically identical with that of Irving Babbitt as expressed in *Literature and the American College* (1908). Whereas Babbitt defended the humanities as central to a liberal education in college, my account will be centered in the high schools as they exist today. The formidable forces that opposed the humanities in Babbitt's time are still with us, and since his death in 1933 many additional developments have contributed to the further decline of the humanities at all levels of American education.

We might begin by identifying the subjects included in a humanities curriculum: history, literature, ancient and modern foreign languages, philosophy and religion, mathematics and the physical sciences, politics and economics, music and the fine arts, and physical education. Since the humanities include the whole range of man's creative achievements within recorded history, everything cultural within the long historical experience that formed the character of Western civilization is a legitimate part of a good humanities program. Ideally, the historical study of Western civilization should begin with the ancient civilizations of the Near East, Greece and Rome, and continue through the Middle Ages, with the Judæo-Christian civilization of Europe, through the Renaissance and the development of modern sci-

ence, the Protestant Reformation, the Enlightenment and nineteenth century, down to the present. (It would be unwise in high
school to pursue strange cultures before knowing Western civilization, so that the study of Oriental cultures should not be
included in the humanities curriculum).

The ideal opening humanities course in high school would be a
survey of Western civilization, its history, literature, institutional
structures, and value system. Such a course should be followed by
one in European history. Ideally, these courses in history should
be taught along with separate courses in literature: English
history with English literature, and American history with American literature, so that the maximum cross-fertilization could
occur. These essential courses should never be amalgamated into
a so-called "interdisciplinary" hybrid entitled "Humanities," as
such attempts to integrate these subjects invariably result in a
superficial program. Each of these subjects should be taught
separately, in the traditional manner, with no gimmicks, fads,
novelties, or concessions to ephemeral interests – only solid, substantial reading matter combined with demanding requirements
in writing.

It should be self-evident that a well-conceived and integrated
high school program in humanities is not possible in practice
unless the philosophy of education which prevails is based upon
faith in the traditional moral, intellectual, social, and æsthetic
normative principles of the liberal arts. In addition, the teachers
must be well-educated in the humanities, supported by the administration, and function in an atmosphere of collegiality, like a
family feeling, with high personal and corporate morale. The
core curriculum of basic subjects would need to be backed by
meaningful academic standards, centered in tests, grading, discipline, and other forms of accountability. Our high schools would
have to recognize that intellectual virtues cannot be measured by
standardized quantitative test scores; much less can character.
To teach the humanities in this spirit is not a Utopian impossi-

bility, nor is it, as some people have contended, an "undemocratic" program, snobbish and holier than thou toward the unwashed proletariat. Teachers of the humanities are not culture vultures dispensing esoteric knowledge to a private body of the elect. If as Matthew Arnold has said, the humanities are "the best that has been said, thought, written, and otherwise expressed about the human experience," the knowledge and civility which the humanities inculcate is valuable to every individual, and available to all who can profit from the full development of their intellectual, moral, social, and æsthetic nature.

I am well aware of the many impediments which prevent the humanities from holding a central place in many American high schools, of the interests and forces which have long neglected the humanities, allowed them to exist in an emasculated form, or eliminated them. A catalogue of the forces opposed to the humanities would include the following: (1) the contradiction and folly which compels students by law to attend school until age sixteen, on the grounds that American democracy requires informed and literate citizens, and then creates a permissive system which allows uneducated students to elect programs that produce graduates who can neither read nor write and who have practically no knowledge of Western civilization or American democracy and few intellectual or cultural interests; (2) the system of teacher certification which is more concerned with methodology than with mastery of the subject to be taught, and which fails to insist upon a high level of general literacy and knowledge in favor of technical specialization; (3) an administrative structure which is more often an end in itself than an instrumental means of education, and which is infatuated with surveys, statistics, descriptive sociological studies of various kinds, and public relations, rather than with the quality of education received by students; (4) the utilitarian-materialist philosophy of life and education, which makes a narrow vocational training the central concern of high schools; (5) ideological theories that our schools are the instruments for solving America's social problems, by creating equality of condition among all students, in order to establish an egalitarian democratic society. These theories, backed by government bureaucratic authority, have reduced many inner city high schools to morally decadent centers of organized anti-intellectual chaos, the triumph of nihilism over meaningful corporate authority or education of almost any kind.

This very limited inventory of the established forces which subordinate or even exclude the humanities in American secondary education is sufficient to note that a serious sickness lies at the heart of many of our high schools, a sickness that requires a prescriptive remedy if we are to restore American education to good health. In some form the basic humanities should be taught to all high school students, as the necessary means of insuring literacy and knowledge of Western civilization. The first two years of high school English should be devoted to such basics as grammar, mechanics, rhetoric, composition, and an introduction to literary genres – fiction as short story and novel, drama, and poetry. Whether or not it is considered "undemocratic" to distinguish between students according to their ability and interests, it is certainly common sense to distinguish them according to their ultimate objectives in education – between those who choose not to go to college and those whose plans include college. A curriculum centered wholly in the humanities should be required during the last two years for college-bound students. It would be wise to include survey courses in English literature and English history during the junior year, and survey courses in American literature and American history during the senior year. I would like to describe and analyze an archetypal model of one such course – in English literature – based upon my own experience as a college student. But before I present my archetypal model in literature I shall make an extensive digression on an effective method by which a high school teacher of literature could approach his subject.

Undoubtedly, one of the most important facts of twentieth century life is the speed and extent of scientific developments, particularly in medicine and technology. Since science in the abstract is regarded in our time with almost superstitious awe by the general public, and dominates so much in the modern world, a high school teacher of literature and the humanities would be well-advised to take advantage of this fact. An excellent strategy to introduce the humanities with no need to be apologetic or defensive is to compare and contrast the so-called "two cultures" embodied in science and the humanities, particularly literature. Attempts to define the right relationship between science and literature have been made with various results by Thomas Henry Huxley and Matthew Arnold in the nineteenth century, and by Sir Arthur Eddington, C. P. Snow, F. R. Leavis, Robert Oppenheimer, Lionel Trilling, and others in the twentieth century. This fact indicates that the relationship between the world of science, which everyone believes is "practical," and the world of literary culture, which many people regard as "impractical," is of perennial importance and interest to highly educated men, and should be understood by high school students.

Many people are convinced that the "iron curtain" which separates the totalitarian Communist world from the free world of parliamentary constitutional government is not as great as the iron curtain that separates the "two cultures" of science and technology as opposed to the ancient Greco-Roman Classical tradition and the art, literature, and culture derived from the Judæo-Christian tradition. Perhaps the primary function of the humanities, both in high school and college, is to enable students to know, understand, penetrate, and remove that cultural iron curtain.

In challenging the acquired prejudice that many high school students have against the humanities, based upon their ignorance or uncritical faith that science holds the solution to every human problem, a teacher could point out that the most outstanding schools of science and technology – such as M.I.T. and Cal Tech – have very extensive programs in the humanities along with science and technology. Students at these schools can even major in history and literature while aiming at careers in professions based upon science. To Bacon's aphorism that scientific "knowledge is power," these schools add Plato's dictum that philosophical "knowledge is virtue." They recognize that pure science, which defines the abstract laws of physical nature, is not enough; that applied science in technology is also not sufficient; nor is it even sufficient to teach that each science has its own laws and is also related to all the other sciences. These schools of science and technology are aware of the multifarious world of man in society. Therefore, they supplement and temper courses in pure and applied science with humanistic courses in history, literature, politics, arts, and languages. In short, they seek actively to bridge the gap between the "two cultures," by insisting upon a close reciprocal relationship between science and human concerns.

A simple way to introduce high school students to think of the differences between science and literature is to distinguish between the total material cosmos and objective world of science, and the total complex inner nature of man – his senses, reason, emotions, will, and imagination, with which literature is chiefly concerned. There is the external open universe of infinite matter to be perceived, and the conscious mind of man as the perceiver. It would be a dull student who would not admit that the role of the self-conscious mind of man as perceiver is of paramount importance. Man is in the universe, but beyond existence or being there is meaning, and as meaning the external universe is in man's mind in his understanding of it. But such meaning can occur only when there is a dynamic relationship, coherence, and unity between mind or spirit and matter. Both science and literature have each their respective literal facts, theories, concepts, symbolic forms, and linguistic symbols, by which the interactions between mind and matter may be explained. It should be noted, however, that there is today no wholly satisfactory hypothesis to explain such interactions.

It may come as a shock to students who revere science to discover that the chief concern of science, the material universe, is in itself without any meaning. Astronomically speaking, the material universe is meaningless until man, as the astronomer, provides meaning to it. As Robert Frost has said in his poem, "Desert Places," the universe, with its "empty spaces/ Between stars – on stars where no human race is," has "no expression, nothing to express." William Blake's "atoms of Democritus and Newton's particles of light" become meaningful only in direct proportion to the power of the human mind which understands them. Bishop Berkeley's "To be is to be perceived" is refined beyond being into meaning by man's intelligence working upon the elements of matter. That is why investigations of material nature are as much studies of man as the perceiving agent of matter as they are of matter itself. In this vital sense, every true scientist is also necessarily a humanist whose conscious mind is engaged in a constant dialogue with atomic matter. The probes into matter of the scientist's mind and the revelations of matter to his mind are what humanize the universe. Conversely, every true humanist also needs to know the basic principles of pure and applied science, both as instrumental means and as an end. The humanist studies the physical sciences in order to understand the laws which govern the operations of matter which scientific studies have revealed.

Having established the different domains of science and literature, the high school teacher of literature is in a strong position to show how science and literature perceive, interpret, and present their respective worlds in very different ways. For example, to a biologist or zoologist, a nightingale is a bird belonging to the

thrush family *Turdidæ*, of the genus *Luscinia*, and the species
megarhynchos. It is about six inches long, russet-brown above,
white-breasted, reddish on the rump and tail, and lives mainly on
insects. Its night song is the result of its digestive system and
mating instinct. But to the poet, such as John Keats, the nightingale is perceived singing within a romantic landscape of moon-
light in a forest setting, and it is a symbol of the great power of
imaginative creativity and the enduring significance of beauty in
art, in contrast to the dull and tragic passing world of man's
ordinary life. Once such a comparison is made, students will
come to see that science and literature provide two very different
ways of viewing the same reality. To their surprise they may also
discover that their approach to the reality of the nightingale is
like that of the poet rather than the scientist, because it includes
normative human values which affect them personally.

The next step in the literary education of the high school
student is for him to discover that so far as science conveys its
meaning through symbols it holds to a literal one-to-one corre-
spondence between its symbols or language and the object or
process it describes. To the scientist two plus two always equals
four and nothing else (on the decimal system), and a rose is a
rose and nothing but a rose, and never a flower symbolizing love,
beauty, or desire. The scientist, as a scientist, is forbidden to go
beyond the one-to-one correlation between the precise, denota-
tive, limited quantitative meaning of a word, because he aims at
absolute accuracy. Any conceptual or emotive significance a rose
may hold in human values is not his province to explore. Unlike
the florist or the poet he cannot "say it with flowers." Nor can
the scientist use the quantitative symbols of science to get at the
human characteristics described by the poet or dramatist: he
cannot tell you the square root of MacBeth's unethical ambition,
and as a scientist he would have to dismiss the witches as
superstitious nonsense, and not consider them as harbingers of
fate. The scientist cannot give us the boiling point of Hamlet's

famous soliloquy. From these necessary limitations of science in dealing with human nature students can learn that any attempt to reduce complex human affairs to any quantitative formula is fraught with dangers and difficulties, and ultimately doomed to failure. This is a very valuable lesson in an age dominated by science. It is important in the intellectual development of high school students that they should acquire a healthy skepticism toward any claim that man's discursive reasoning processes – inductive, deductive, or analytical – can arrive at final answers to anything that involves the human spirit. Once a student understands that excessive rationalism is not reasonable, that we can't translate simple logic into complex life, he can more readily learn to appreciate the unique role of literature and the humanities in his education.

For the poet, in contrast to the scientist, linguistic symbols operate not literally but metaphorically. They are open-ended, filled with implications, ambiguities, unresolved contraries. Through their associations with other words and symbols in their context they may acquire multiple possible meanings. For the poet, as with God in the fourth gospel, "In the beginning was the Word . . . ." If God is said to write straight with crooked lines, the poet too by indirections finds directions out. As Robert Frost said in his essay "Education by Poetry," "Poetry provides the one permissible way of saying one thing and meaning another." The metaphors of poetry run the whole range from trivial thought "to the profoundest thinking that we have." Frost went on to say, the "greatest of all attempts to say one thing in terms of another is the philosophical attempt to say matter in terms of spirit, or spirit in terms of matter, to make the final unity." The poet knows that the multiple meanings, ambiguities, paradoxes, ironies, and mysteries of life cannot be reduced to any formula or scientific laws. The world of literature includes the comic, the tragic, the pathetic, the sentimental, the divine and the profane, the sublime and the beautiful, the idealistic and the starkly realistic, the inner and outer life of men and women, in the strange uncategorical meaning of human existence. Through compressed symbols, images, analogies, metaphors, and the rich arsenal of his linguistic tools or weapons, the poet provides succinctly in unforgettable fresh forms, in brilliant phrases, and in magical harmonies indelibly stamped on the mind, what cannot be said in tomes of factual scientific evidence and discursive logical arguments.

For the process of literary creativity is a continual process of intuitional self-discovery and revelation. The poet does not merely express thematic ideas or sentiments through images and symbols. A poem is never merely an instrumental means to something else. It is first its own inherent reason for being. Archibald MacLeish is quite right that "A poem should not mean/But be." This is so because like God in the original creation of the universe the poet transubstantiates chaotic matter into enduring form. He brings into existence something that did not exist before he created his poem, shapes it into a coherent and orderly form, and creates a supreme fiction that possesses a kind of temporal immortality. The poet's work is not ephemeral, like that of the journalist or historian, but becomes a monument of enduring intellect that endures and holds significance for many generations of men and women. A poem brings verbal and sensory order to our chaotic world of passing and disconnected sense impressions, rational perceptions, and emotive feelings. In Frost's words, a poem is "a momentary stay against confusion." T. S. Eliot said much the same thing: that poetry enables humanity to "shore up our ruins."

From all that I have said it should be clear that the real antithesis is not between science and literature or humanistic culture, but between two qualities of mind and temper in human nature. If there is a split between "two cultures," it is between that species of persons who are literal-minded fundamentalists, totally lacking in any sense of metaphor or æsthetic and moral imagination, and the opposite kind of persons who at once respect facts yet have the imagination and sensitivity to perceive reality through metaphors, images, symbols, and myths. As a human being a scientist is as capable of understanding and appreciating art, music, and poetry as a poet or humanist. The literal-minded person is chained to the dictionary meaning of words. His virtue in language is limited to the black letter of the law. He lacks the audacity released by the verbal imagination, and is deficient in the sense of play in a drama, the sensibility of emotion in a lyric, or the metaphorical dimensions of events in a narrative. Such a person is like an academic grammarian, fond of abstract definitions, rigid rules, and frozen syntax, but incapable of dealing with the salt and tang of colloquial idioms and speech. There is a literary fundamentalism as stultifying as religious fundamentalism. Education in literature can help a high school student to overcome such deficiencies in language, and open and intensify his æsthetic and moral imagination. With these words I now end my digression on an effective method for approaching literature in a high school humanities curriculum, and turn to my archetypal model of a two semester survey course in English literature.

My archetypal model is the freshman survey of English literature taught at Middlebury College during the 1940's, by far the best course in literature that I ever had. I do not suggest that any high school should teach such a course, although on a reduced scale, with proper consideration of differences in circumstances between a liberal arts freshman course and high school English, it could be taught to a selected group of high school students as part of their preparation for college. Nor is there any merit to the objection that such a course is too difficult for high school students. Robert Frost is right in saying that metaphorical language runs the range from trivial thought "to the profoundest thinking that we have," so that high school students can understand imaginative literature according to the degree of maturity they have achieved. There is no justification in substituting the comics for the classics just to bring education to a common level of understanding. If students have been taught imaginative literature beginning in grade school, starting with *Mother Goose* and Robert Louis Stevenson's *A Child's Garden of Verses*, with Grimm's fairy stories and Aesop's fables, etc., they would have developed gradually in their ability to handle more demanding literature, so that by the time they are juniors in high school they should be ready to profit from a survey of English literature. I would urge that this course should be taught in conjunction with a separate survey course in English and European history, for the maximum in cross-fertilization. The historical perspective that accompanies such survey courses is enormously valuable in providing students with a sense of the unbroken traditions of culture in Western civilization. The survey courses in English literature should not be in literary history, but in literary criticism of the assigned poems, plays, and fiction.

The survey course in English literature at Middlebury College covered selected essential literature from Beowulf through Thomas Hardy. The basic text was an anthology of prose and poetry in two large volumes. This was supplemented by three plays by Shakespeare – a history, a tragedy, and a comedy – while for biography we read Boswell's *Life of Samuel Johnson*. For fiction, Fielding's *Joseph Andrews* was read for the eighteenth century; Dickens' *Great Expectations* for the nineteenth century; and Virginia Woolf's *To the Lighthouse* for the twentieth century. For general literary history, criticism, and a traditional literary vocabulary, we consulted as needed Thrall and Hibbard's *A Handbook of English Literature*.

After the opening orientation lectures by Professor Harry Owen, most meetings of the class were conducted in the Socratic method, with the students taking an active part in discussing the reading assignments in the literature. Since almost every reading assignment was accompanied by a writing assignment on a particular poem, play, essay, or novel, the students came to class well-prepared, with their minds sharply focussed upon their subject, ready to defend a thesis. Almost three times each week for two semesters students had to submit a brief critical paper on a poem or play, an essay or novel, or on some conflict of interpretation or æsthetic problem that had arisen during class discussion. Occasionally, students were encouraged to write imitations of a poem, such as a Shakespearean sonnet, or a lyric by Donne, Keats, or Tennyson, or a dramatic monologue by Browning. These assignments were called "writing from models," a much more demanding and less pretentious method than so-called "creative writing." Writing about the literature *before* discussing it in class compelled each student to look to his own critical resources in handling the literature, rather than being a polly parrot of the teacher. Often a student would be called upon in class to read and defend his paper. He soon learned that pretentious or abstract rhetoric, or a mere spilling out of his emotions over a poem, were not acceptable techniques. Students soon learned to concentrate upon the elements in a work of literature, upon the structure, the large units of which it was composed, how these parts were related to each other to form a coherent whole or unity, and what each part contributed to the unfolding theme or meaning. Attention also had to be paid to the literary techniques, to the dramatic situation and plot in a play, to the function of its setting; to diction, images, symbols, rhyme, rhythm, and meter in a poem; to the point-of-view or angle of vision and the traits and relationships of characters in a novel. We soon learned how greatly these literary devices shaped the theme or meaning of a work. In a course such as this there was no separate need for remedial reading. To round out the reading, writing, and class discussions, each student had regularly assigned conferences with the teacher, to discuss any particular problems in the course.

In addition to providing an extensive knowledge of English

literature in all its genres, and creating a sense of self-discipline
in reading and writing habits, a good survey course in English
literature reveals the vital historical changes and continuities in
English and European thought and values, from the early mediæval period to modern times. It becomes crystal clear to any
aware student that the world view of the Judæo-Christian religion, backed by the Classical Greek and Roman civil-social order
and culture, and the philosophy of Plato, Aristotle, and the
Stoics, provided the unchallenged basis for Western civilization
and culture for over fifteen centuries. The education of Europeans during these centuries was centered in the humanities. But
with the emergence of such men as Roger Bacon (1214?-1294?),
whose *Opus Majus* (Greater Work) was sent to Pope Clement IV
in 1266, the fields of anatomy, optics, philology, and alchemy
were opened, and modern science began to develop. Here, in
helping the student of literature to understand the enormous
significance of the "new philosophy" of science, the intellectual
historian can provide the background necessary to illuminate the
great themes of English literature during the sixteenth and seventeenth centuries.

By the early seventeenth century the speculative theories and
experiments of such scientists as Bacon revolutionized man's
whole conception of the physical universe, and man's relationship to the cosmos, culminating in the revolutionary change from
the Ptolemaic to the Copernican hypothesis. In the process of
studying this revolutionary change, students of English literature
would become aware of the incredible, many-sided genius of
Leonardo da Vinci (1452-1519), perhaps the most perfect repre-
sentative of the humanities in all Western civilization. They
would also become familiar with the essential achievements of
Copernicus (1473-1543), whose great work, *Concerning the Revolutions of the Celestial Spheres* (1543), made possible the plane-
tary laws of Tycho Brahe (1546-1601), and Johannes Kepler
(1571-1630), and the telescopic discoveries of Galileo Galilei

(1564-1642), which in turn provided Sir Isaac Newton (1642-1727) with the knowledge necessary to invent a new system of calculus, and to discover the principles of motion and gravitation set forth in his *Philosophia Naturalis Principia Mathematica* (1687). A survey course in English literature should teach students that there were two great traditions upon which the "new philosophy" was based: the empirical-experimental inductive tradition of Francis Bacon (1561-1626), in his *The Advancement of Learning* (1605), and *Novum Organum* (1620), and the scientific rationalism and deductive logic of René Descartes (1596-1650), whose *Discourse on Method* (1637), provided the mathematical basis and quantitative analysis which was to dominate scientific thought for over two centuries, and profoundly affect studies in the humanities.

English literature reveals that the destruction by the new science of astronomy of the world view held by Europeans for over 1,500 years did not occur without considerable spiritual anguish and intellectual anxiety. Early in the seventeenth century, John Donne (1571?-1631), in a celebrated passage in his poem, "An Anatomie of the World," described the sense of alienation and fear felt by men in perceiving the shift from the old established Ptolemaic system, with the earth at the center of the universe, and its displacement in the "new philosophy" of the Copernican system:

> And new philosophy calls all in doubt,
> The Element of fire is quite put out;
> The sun is lost, and th'earth, and no man's wit
> Can well direct him where to looke for it.
> And surely men confess that this world's spent
> When in the Planets, and the Firmament
> They seek so many new; they see that this
> Is crumbled out againe to his Atomies.
> 'Tis all in peeces, all coherence gone;
> All just supply, and all Relation.

This vital passage clearly reflects the beginnings of what T. S. Eliot called the "divided sensibility" that characterizes the alienation of modern man – that terrible separation between his emotional life centered in religion, the arts, and humanities, and his intellectual life centered in science, which foreshadowed the deep breach in the "two cultures." The "new philosophy" which "calls all in doubt" was extended to religion, law, politics, and every branch of human studies. The implications of this revolutionary change were not lost upon John Milton. He sensed this conflict so profoundly, that although he was personally convinced by the Copernican hypothesis, in *Paradise Lost* he retained the cosmology of the Ptolemaic system as more in harmony with the meaningful moral and spiritual order of Christianity.

It is worth noting that practically all of these scientists of the sixteenth and seventeenth centuries were educated in the humanities, that most of them were highly orthodox in their religion, and that there were not "two cultures" to separate them from their earlier intellectual and moral traditions. Late in the seventeenth century John Dryden, the foremost poet, dramatist, and literary critic of his age, and a thoroughly orthodox Christian, had no difficulty in harmonizing his literary achievements and religion with the new science. He was an active member of the Royal Society, and headed up a commission to bring the English language into harmony with its scientific experiments. In *An Essay of Dramatic Poesy* (written 1666, published 1668), Dryden noted the conflict between the ancients and the moderns (which is at the heart of the separation of the "two cultures"), but he paid great tribute to the achievements of science up to his time:

> Is it not evident, in these last hundred years, when the study of philosophy has been the business of all the Virtuosi in Christendom, that almost a new nature has been revealed to us? That more errors of the school have been detected, more useful experiments in philosophy have been made, more noble secrets in optics, medicine, anatomy, astronomy, discovered, than in all those credulous

and doting ages from Aristotle to us? – so true it is, that nothing spreads more fast than science, when rightly and generally cultivated.

Although a latent or potential antagonism between the physical sciences and religion and the humanities was evident almost from the beginning, science was not regarded as an adversary to religion and culture until the eighteenth-century "Enlightenment." Denis Diderot (1713-1784), and his twenty-eight volume *Encyclopedie* (1751-1765), made war upon the established religious orthodoxy, and did much to separate science from the Classical- Judæo-Christian culture of Europe.

The conflict precipitated between the "two cultures" during the eighteenth century is still with us today. It was intensified in the nineteenth century by Darwinian evolutionary theory. It is worth noting that Charles Darwin, in his autobiography, makes it clear that the more he became immersed in scientific observations and studies the less positive feeling he had for the plays of Shakespeare, or the poetry of Milton or Wordsworth. The unfortunate antithesis between science and literature and the humanities inherited from the "Enlightenment" has further intensified the "divided sensibility" of modern man, and has led to a much deeper alienation. This is very evident in the expanded application of the scientific method in human affairs and humane studies, which has resulted in history being displaced by value-free, descriptive sociology, philosophy by psychology and linguistics, and literature by journalism. The expanded penetration of science into art is perhaps most evident in modern abstract art. It is clear that the on-going revolution in the developments in theoretical and applied science cannot be limited to material concerns, but vitally affects the whole of man's life in society. The application of the scientific method to human affairs has put the whole religious-humanistic tradition on the defensive, and threatens its extinction in education. The humanities have not humanized the physical sciences so much as the sciences have mechanized the humanities, and made them appear to be obsolete. A survey course in English literature, combined with studies in intellectual history, can illuminate how these vital changes have occurred since the seventeenth century, and can provide historical perspective and intellectual understanding of the values and normative principles which have been lost to mankind in Western culture.

For example, one of the most valuable principles of Classical literary criticism – that there are valid objective standards by which to judge a work of literary art – has been wholly lost to contemporary men and women who believe that all literary judgments are wholly private, subjective, arbitrary, and solipsistic. Perhaps the most perfect expression in all English literature of a belief in objective æsthetic norms, to be found in the permanently enduring literary works of Western culture, from Homer to the present, is in these lines from Pope's *Essay on Criticism*:

> First follow Nature, and your judgment frame
> By her just standard, which is still the same:
> Unerring Nature, still divinely bright,
> One clear, unchanged, and universal light,
> Life, force, and beauty, must to all impart,
> At once the source, and end, and test of art.

To "follow Nature" is to *discover* normative literary standards, not to *create* them. Such standards are not merely useful: they are true. They are not a product of someone's private, nihilistic, decadent ideology. The highest models of excellence in poetry are to be found in the long-established literary traditions that in Western civilization reach back to Virgil and Homer. Following these models does not prevent originality: every good poet can "snatch a grace beyond the reach of art." But the best poems from the past provide standards of comparison by which to measure the creative productions of contemporary poets. For a literary tradition is not merely a bucket of ashes; it is not the dead hand of the past stultifying the vital and living present, as some "Romantic" writers have asserted, out of their parochialism of time. As Samuel Johnson has said, so much of what passes for originality is mere ignorance of our ancestors. In his essay, "Tradition and the Individual Talent," T. S. Eliot showed that only by mastering the living tradition of past literature can a contemporary writer fulfill his originality. Objective standards applied to a close study of a work of literature precede comparative studies, which in turn can open up insights into all of the arts and other humanities. For example, a student who perceives that John Dryden's loose heroic couplets become tight and closed in Pope's poems, a passion for form and order, may in time find parallels in the minuets and classical symphonies of Haydn and Mozart, and further counterparts in the formal gardens of Versailles.

One of the highlights of a survey course in English literature is Jonathan Swift's *Gulliver's Travels* (1726). It is an ideal work of fiction to teach on almost any level of education, because it can be understood on at least three levels of meaning: (1) as a children's fairy story or fictional fantasy; (2) as a fictional satire on early eighteenth-century English society and politics; (3) as a universal satire on the intellectual, moral, and social weaknesses of human nature, screened through the fatuous optimism of Gulliver. On each of these three levels of meaning *Gulliver's Travels* is at once very simple and clear, in its plot narrative and prose style, and yet filled with profound symbolic significances that illuminate the moral imagination of its readers. Through the use of verisimilitude in factual details, Swift establishes Gulliver's integrity as a truthful narrator, and thus creates an illusion of probability that breaks down the psychic distance readers normally have toward fantasies and fictions, and converts the "willing suspension of disbelief" in readers into faith in the truth of the narrative, as though it were a factual account of Gulliver's personal history and experience. It is small wonder that one fundamentalist-minded reader, on being asked what he thought of *Gulliver's Travels*, is said to have responded: "I don't believe a word of it."

Another obvious value in teaching a survey course in English literature is that it can expose students to the full range of literary styles and genres, and thus improve their taste. Both in high school and among undergraduates in college, literary taste tends to be crude and undeveloped. Invariably, such students prefer the "Romantics" to any other period of literature. They are often filled to overflowing with a vague, sententious, unfocused, so-called moral idealism, and with an emotional sensibility that favors a pantheistic view of the universe. They have a burning yearning for the high ineffable, an urge to merge with the universe in soaring, sentimental, ersatz effusions. These feelings pass for æsthetic spirituality with them, and they are quick to respond to poems which have a direct appeal to their emotions, such as this pantheistic passage from Walt Whitman:

> What do you think has become of the young and old men?
> And what do you think has become of the women and
> 　children?

> They are alive and well somewhere,
> The smallest sprout shows there is really no death,
> And if ever there was it led forward life, and does not wait at
> 　the end to arrest it,

> And ceas'd the moment life appear'd.

> All goes onward and outward, nothing collapses,
> And to die is different from what anyone supposed, and
> 　luckier.

The final lines of William Cullen Bryant's "Thanatopsis" are of a similar kind:

> So live, that when thy summons comes to join
> The innumerable caravan, which moves
> To that mysterious realm, where each shall take
> His chamber in the silent halls of death,
> Thou go not, like the quarry-slave at night,
> Scourged to his dungeon, but, sustained and soothed
> By an unfaltering trust, approach thy grave
> Like one who wraps the drapery of his couch
> About him, and lies down to pleasant dreams.

I would let high school students and undergraduates disport themselves with such poetry, in the faith that in time the better students will outgrow it, and with a more mature taste will be gathered into the artifice of monuments of enduring intellect.

I agree with Robert Frost that the essential function of a high school teacher of literature is to create "disciplined enthusiasm" for short stories, novels, plays, and poems. Never mind that some of the enthusiasm is crude and tasteless: a better appreciation of better literature will follow in due time. Frost maintained that there were at least five things a good teacher could have students do with a poem in the classroom: (1) read it out loud; (2) reread it; (3) memorize it; (4) write it into a student's anthology of poems; and (5) discuss it by applying its theme or meaning to life in a story or analogy with something within the student's experience, with an eye to enlarging or illuminating his experience. Frost believed that we should never underestimate the importance of simply reading a poem out loud. A good reading requires the skills of an actor, and is as much a performing art as playing music, singing, or acting on the stage. A bad reading, which ignores the meter, rhythm, rhyme, and phonetic pattern of a poem, or stumbles over the punctuation and pronunciation of words, or is delivered in a monotone, without dramatic emphasis, reveals weaknesses in reading comprehension, which a second or subsequent reading may correct. Memorizing a poem requires a deeper concentration upon the sequence of images and associative patterns of sense appeals, and the unfolding inductive or deductive logic in the poem, and this added discipline in the art of good reading develops sensitivity to language as diction, as phraseology, and as coherent structure. The complex relationship between what Frost called "the sound of meaning and the meaning of sound" is intensified and clarified through memory work. This process is further confirmed by writing a poem in a notebook, and a collection of such poems selected by the student becomes a record of his taste and development in understanding literature. Finally, for a student to apply a poem to his understanding of life is to make it a permanent part of his living literary culture, so that literature is not regarded as an esoteric subject, hermetically sealed off from daily living. In perceiving the world of poetry, a value-centered fictional world of good order, a student may be psychologically conditioned to understand life better long after he has forgotten particular poems.

It is worth noting that Frost's list of things a teacher can do with a poem did not include critical analysis. Like William Blake he feared that "we murder to dissect." Yet we cannot assume that high school students will begin with a valid or intellectually defensable æsthetic theory or conception of the nature of literary art, and therefore for someone unskilled in the metaphorical uses of language a rational awareness of the elements of a poem may be useful as preliminary to a more profound intuitional or imaginative understanding. Without a valid theory of art and sound principles of practical criticism, both teachers and students are often reduced to vague, subjective, emotive responses, disconnected impressionistic and arbitrary comments, without point or substance, and with no illumination of the poem, play, or novel. I have known high school teachers of literature to resort to pathetic parlor games because they don't know what to do with a work of literature. Practical criticism has a necessary claim upon such teachers.

The most basic principle of practical criticism is that the teacher must deal directly with a particular work, and treat it primarily as an æsthetic art object. A teacher who concentrates upon the structure, techniques, and thematic content of a work will keep biography at a minimum, omit literary history, avoid the intentional fallacy and the affective fallacy, and steer clear of applying ideological theories, such as Marxism and Freudianism, to the literary work. There is no fixed formula for practical literary criticism. But an analysis of the structure, of such large units as stanzas in a poem, or act and scenes in a play, of chapters or groups of chapters in a novel, will provide a sense of how the parts of a work relate to each other to form a coherent and unified whole. In teaching literature in high school a teacher should avoid the purely technical elements in a piece as much as possible. Yet through a functional approach that goes beyond making a mere inventory of the basic elements, a teacher can show how good technique advances the theme or meaning of a poem, how the phonetic pattern of rhyme, meter, rhythm, and diction, as well as the images, metaphors, and symbols, create and convey the mood or tone and meaning. In discussing the content or meaning of a poem the great danger is the heresy of paraphrase. We must never give students the false impression that a prose summary of a poem, however accurate and thorough, is the equivalent of the poem. A poem is always more than the good prose it might have been. Knowledge of literature is important, but the deepest understanding of literature underscores its value and significance, and these can best be attained by a sound æsthetic theory and skill in practical criticism.

As an example of how literature can be taught to high school students in a survey course I would like to analyze Frost's poem, "Stopping by Woods on a Snowy Evening":

Whose woods these are I think I know.
His house is in the village though;
He will not see me stopping here
To watch his woods fill up with snow.

My little horse must think it queer
To stop without a farmhouse near
Between the woods and frozen lake
The darkest evening of the year.

He gives his harness bells a shake
To ask if there is some mistake.
The only other sound's the sweep
Of easy wind and downy flake.

The woods are lovely, dark and deep,
But I have promises to keep,
And miles to go before I sleep,
And miles to go before I sleep.

This lyric monologue has a very simple and clear dramatic situation, within the common human experience of every reader. The brief plot action consists of the speaker, probably a man, on his way home on a snowy winter night in a single horse-drawn sled. He stops to admire the beauty of the snow falling in the dark mysterious woods. The restlessness of his horse cuts across the almost hypnotic mood in the speaker, created by the soft wind and snowflakes, and reminds him, regretfully, that he must leave the scene and return to the practical needs of home and society. The images in this poem, which create the setting, dramatic situation, action, and mood, are all simple, and the diction is so colloquial and idiomatic that not one word would cause any difficulty in comprehension.

The structure of the poem is like the dramatic situation. It consists of four stanzas, each one a quatrain of exactly four iambic tetrameter lines, rhyming AABA. The organic unity, mood, and variety in the poem are achieved in the phonetic pattern of the structure – in the regular meter and varied rhythm, in the interlocking rhyme scheme by which the unrhymed third line in each stanza becomes the rhymed lines in the next stanza, until the final quatrain, where the third line repeats the rhyme scheme and the whole line is repeated in the last line.

The repetition of the final lines becomes an incantation, and lifts the whole poem to a metaphorical dimension which opens it to several interpretations of the theme. In the final line the "miles" of the road to be traveled by the speaker can refer simultaneously to the literal number of miles he must travel that night to reach home and metaphorically to the miles he must travel down the road of life before reaching the "sleep" of death. Some critics have discovered a Freudian subconscious "death wish" in the speaker, with each image of the poem assuming symbolic significance accordingly. Clearly, the great difference between a man and a horse in appreciating the æsthetic elements in nature is another possible theme. Or the setting, character, and action may be regarded as creating a mood poem whose theme cannot be ascertained in rational terms. Or the poem may be seen as stating an antithesis between the claims of æsthetic nature and the practical obligations and claims of human nature in society. Only imaginative literature, with its metaphorical uses of language, can contain such a rich array of meaning in such a simple form.

Finally, a good example of a short fiction admirably suited for high school students is Mark Twain's "The Celebrated Jumping Frog of Caloveras County," which Frost regarded as the most perfect short story of its kind in all American literature. Frost called Twain's jumping frog story "a poem in prose fiction," because in the monologue of the narrator the voice tones and senses of sound in the style and Western frontier idiom are as lyrical as in a poem. The prose literally sings. The images are sharp and original. The diction is simple. The timing in the punch lines is perfect: there is punch in the punch lines, as in all good anecdotes and narratives.

The structure is a story within a story, in which the original narrator becomes the listener, like the reader, until the very end, when he pulls everything together. This envelope technique compels the student to give thought to both the narrator and the listener. The simple plot, well within anyone's common experience, describes how the country bumpkin's champion frog, named Dan'l Webster, leaped free and far until the city slicker filled him secretly with buckshot, after which he was heavy and ponderous, anchored to the earth like a solid building, and easily outjumped by just an ordinary frog. The story fulfills the great classical principle that good literature at once gives pleasure and provides a richer understanding of life. The theme, centered in the plot, reveals how a shrewd country con man and inveterate gambler is conned by an even more shrewd city slicker con man. Without any critical analysis at all, students can enjoy the sheer comedy of the dramatic situation, and perceive in the reversal of the roles of the two protagonists a kind of rough justice. There are no obscure philosophical allusions or challenging intellectual concepts or esoteric symbols to baffle or turn off even students of ordinary sensibility or literary interests.

And yet, despite its surface simplicity, Twain's story is a literary parable whose deeper metaphorical or symbolic meaning can be unfolded by a good teacher. Even on the level of plot the jumping frog story illustrates how creative art works. For the mundane student who wants trite truisms, thumb-nail summaries of the theme or meaning of a story, the teacher can provide a few such aphorisms that can be derived from the tall tale: "Appearances are deceiving." "Look before you leap." "Pride cometh before a fall." Or closer to the plot, "it takes one to know one," meaning it takes a better con man to con a con man. After such initial banalities the teacher can ask the students to make their own aphorisms of the parable. This is an easy way to encourage students to interpret a story. On a higher level of meaning the teacher can ask the students to apply the story to something within their own experience or understanding of life. Frost himself used the story to compare the characteristics of the poet with those of the scholar. Before the frog was filled with buckshot he was like a poet, light and imaginative and capable of great leaps by a command or the slightest stimulus. But after being filled with buckshot the frog was like a scientific critic or scholar, weighted down, stuffed with ponderous knowledge and heavy logic, but useless in the art of jumping. No amount of prodding could get him to budge. The chief virtues of the poet – imagination, fancy, audacity, courage, wit, and humor, which created his originality – were lost. As Frost remarked: "No performance, no form." The chief characteristics of the scholar are a love of facts for their own sake as knowledge, and for thoroughness, accuracy, and systematic scientific method. Compared to poets, most scholars lack imagination and spontaneity and are "humorless and witless." Scholars are "too thorough, too specialized, too fastidious, too proud." In summary, Frost said the scholar sticks to his subject until he is stuck to his subject. He exhausts everything about his subject until everything about it exhausts him and everything else. His knowledge clings to him like burrs caught in crossing a field. But the poet allows his subject to stick to him as long as he wishes, and while it is attached to him he shoots out leads from it which he is free to follow. The poet keeps up a fast moving interest in his subject while getting the maximum benefit of what his subject has to offer. This is the main difference between the artist and the scholar and scientist. From this analogy Frost stated a basic personal conviction: there are dangers in absorbing knowledge beyond one's capability to use it well.

Once the jumping frog story has been well discussed, a good teacher can open the discussion into the nature of fictional parables as a basic literary technique in much more complex literature, as a way of conveying important meanings about human nature and life. It might be useful to point out, in passing, that Christ spoke to the people in parables, and that without parables he did not speak to them. Like the poet, He said spirit in terms of matter, in such parables as that of the good Samaritan. The jumping frog story could be perceived as a first cousin to Aesop's fables. Finally, the teacher could show that *all* imaginative literature works much the same way on a much more complex level – the plays of Shakespeare, and such good American novels which they will read in their survey of American literature as Hawthorne's *The Scarlet Letter* and Twain's *Huckleberry Finn*.

It is clearly no easy task to bridge the gap between the personal, subjective, mysterious inner life of the human mind and spirit, and the objective facts and laws of the physical universe which is the special world of science, and the social universe where the human drama of life is played out. But a humanized social landscape and universe require that some harmony and synthesis between spirit and matter must occur, and this is the great purpose of the humanities. The flow of knowledge between the "two cultures" must be mutual, and good high school teachers of literature and the humanities will make their students aware of the importance of the humanities in a world dominated by the sciences. We must supplement "Knowledge is power" with "Knowledge is moral wisdom." The better that we, as Americans, can produce humanistically educated people the greater will be our culture and civilization. If this humanizing process of redeeming the times begins early, in grade school, every high school student will achieve some degree of æsthetic and intellectual culture, and the moral imagination of the nation will be raised. I believe that our better high school students will respond positively to a well-organized and well-taught program in literature and the humanities. They will be a large saving remnant to strengthen and preserve American civilization. For this we shall need far better humanistically educated teachers than we now have. The main objective of the humanities in high school is to provide substantial overall knowledge of Western civilization, but with considerable regard to the basic principles of each humanistic subject. The development of the critical faculty and good taste will come after high school, in and beyond college. But for a student to acquire a seamless comprehensive philosophy rich enough to encompass the world of science and technology, and the social world, a balanced education in all of the humanities is necessary.

In the preface to the English edition of Élie Halévy's classic, *The Growth of Philosophic Radicalism* (1928), A. D. Lindsay noted "how deeply the Benthamites were influenced by their belief in the possibilities of applying to the study of man and society the principles and methods of the physical sciences. That is the clue to some of the most curious abberations of their thought, and to much of their short-sightedness. The belief is still with us. It is curious how often men are still found to argue in the manner of Bentham that if certain things are admitted to be true, sociology could not be an exact science, and therefore the admissions must not be made." Professor Lindsay's criticism of Benthamite utilitarianism and the pseudo-science of sociology was made in 1928. But it applies in 1988 to all modern positivist thinking which assumes that the principles and methods of the physical sciences can be applied with equal validity to human nature and human affairs in society, including psychology, education, and politics. We are all familiar with the attempts by behavioralists to treat political philosophy and social studies as an exact science, to remain objective, disinterested, detached, impartial observers, stating descriptive facts but never making moral or intellectual normative judgments, in effect to deny any relationship between politics and ethics. What has resulted from such a pseudo-science? We have mountains of dry-as-dust sta-

tistics, quantitative reports galore, mathematical graphs which
point to vacuums, diagnostic charts of factual data, analytical
impressionistic commentaries, etc. Our social scientists are en-
slaved by isolated or synthesized bare facts, which stand like
bleached gravestones or mausoleums in the wasteland of modern
civilization. Theirs is the new scholasticism. The speculative
theological theories of the Mediæval schoolmen were dynamic
and alive, compared with the pointless dead studies of many of
our present-day social scientists. Until there is a return to the
humanistic tradition of political and social studies we can expect
the dehumanizing of mankind to continue.

An emphasis on history in the curriculum of a good high
school humanities program is particularly important. An historical sense is essential for the development of the moral imagination. That is why history should not be taught merely as a
chronology of dynastic or political events, of wars and revolutions, with their military defeats or victories, not even as a series
of cause and effect relationships in human affairs. Intellectual
history is the humanistic core of all historical studies. Students
must be taught to comprehend the important and enduring
principles embodied in events, in discoveries and explorations, in
systems of laws and manners, in theories of society and government, and in humanistic culture and science. The threads of
continuity as well as the disruptions of change are a vital part of
the history of the human race. A sense of history includes not
only a perception of the past, but of the living past in the present,
particularly of the moral and cultural norms which have been
transmitted by religion and the arts, and the legal and political
norms in the continuity of organized society, linking the generations of men and women beyond any merely empirical-rational
account of temporal events. History thus perceived rests upon a
providential view of reality, and incorporates intellectual norms
similar to the moral norms of revealed religion, and is part of the
"right reason" of the natural law. To Edmund Burke history was

a preceptor of moral prudence revealed in "the known march of the ordinary providence of God." Within the American tradition, Abraham Lincoln held much the same view of history. No one can read Lincoln's second inaugural address, and other of his writings, without being made aware that he held a providential view of history. In a good humanities program the role of history is paramount because it creates and maintains a sense of the cultural continuity in Western civilization, and provides a comparative basis between the past achievements and failures of mankind. This undercuts the fictional fantasies of ideological theorists who claim that their systems promise Utopia at the end of historical time. Comparative history against the backdrop of revealed religion also destroys belief in the idea of progress as a law of history, a faith that militates against the study of the humanities, because it regards the past as dead or without value. The whole frame of reference within which all education in America functions is Western civilization from the ancient world of the Near East, Greece, and Rome, to the present. A knowledge of that world through history makes contemporary America most meaningful, and every high school student needs that knowledge to be truly educated.

PERMANENCE AND THE
HISTORY CURRICULUM

Solveig Eggerz

IN EDUCATION, as in other areas, we like to assume all is well, right up to the moment when the appalling evidence crosses our desk, telling us that something entirely different has been the case. The rosy picture was but a cherished illusion.

Thus, we assume that history still holds its rightful place of honor in the schools because it used to be there, more or less, when we went to school. We assume it is there because, as taxpayers, we have been promised that history is a component part of social studies. Alas, this is just barely the case. Not only does history occur infrequently within the curriculum, but where it does appear it does so in the downgraded role of handmaiden to the social sciences. History has not only lost its place in the schools, but it has been cannibalized by social studies.

In the following pages we shall explore some of the philosophies behind this development, as well as how these philosophies work to shape the social studies curriculum. Finally, we shall examine the consequences this holds for students, as well as for our democratic society.

First, let us consider these statistics from a recent survey conducted by the National Assessment of Education Progress. Two-thirds of eleventh graders cannot place the Civil War within the period 1850–1900. One-third does not know that the Declaration of Independence was signed between 1750 and 1800. One-third did not know that Columbus sailed for the New World before 1750. Half could not locate the half century in which World War I occurred. Half did not recognize the names of Winston Churchill or Joseph Stalin. The NAEP survey also showed that many thirteen and seventeen year olds do not know what happens to a law after it passes Congress, and that the majority does not know that a President cannot declare a law unconstitutional.

A 1979 Gallup Poll reported that only three per cent of the nation's seventeen and eighteen year olds could correctly identify Alaska and Hawaii as the last states to join the Union.

Equally interesting is students' ignorance of history's sister subject, geography. "We have a situation where Johnny not only doesn't know how to read or add, he doesn't even know where he is." I quote from James Vining, executive director of the National Council for Geographic Education. Let's consider the degree to which Johnny doesn't know where he is. Ninety-five per cent of university students in North Carolina who took a basic geography test in the fall of 1985 failed it. Among the questions asked:

"What is the approximate 1980 population of the United States?"

"Name the two largest states in area."

"In what countries are these cities located?   (a) Baghdad (b) Lisbon (c) Madras (d) Manila (e) Cape Town (f) Budapest."

Only one of 340 University of Georgia students who took a geography test correctly labeled forty points on a world map. Many of the same students think Canada is a state. About twenty per cent of American students cannot find the United States on a world map, according to results of a test administered to twelve year olds in eight nations by the Dallas *Times Herald* in 1983.

The reason for these typically mediocre test results is not shrouded in mystery. They are not due to the changing nature of our school population, or to the thinning out of the ozone layer, but simply to students' lack of exposure to history as well as geography. Students used to study history in every year of school.

Today the picture is very different. Let's trace the history of the disappearance of history.

In 1899 a committee of the American Historical Association recommended a four-year history curriculum which was adopted in public schools across the land. In the first year of high school, students learned ancient history; in the second, mediæval and modern European history; in the third, English history; and in the fourth, American history and government. The foundation for these studies was laid in elementary schools where students read biographies, mythology, legends and hero tales.

About twenty-five years ago high school students still studied one year of world history and one year of American history. Today most study only one year of American history. The slot that history used to fill is now taken up by contemporary issues and self-awareness exercises, taught under the label of social studies.

The de-emphasis on history in the high schools, when history courses were compressed into a one-year requirement, led to its near disappearance from the elementary schools. What students do learn comes from what Education Secretary William J. Bennett has called, "an odd, amorphous grab bag – derived from such disciplines as anthropology, sociology, law, psychiatry, history, science, economics and geography."

Social studies for the very young capitalize on, rather than transcend, the egocentrism which dominates the lives of children in the early grades. Under a sequence called "expanding environments" a pattern has been established for use in curricula across the country, whereby the child is placed at the center of the universe.

The basic subject of kindergarten social studies is *Me*; first grade, family; second, neighborhood; third, communities. Perhaps social scientists who prepare these curricula are underestimating children's ability to comprehend stories from the past, for teachers report that young children are weary of community helpers and such, having covered this material thoroughly in pre-school. But they become quite enthusiastic at the introduction of a hero from history. This, however, is beyond the curriculum.

In a typical curriculum, state history may be offered in fourth grade and American history in the fifth; followed by more history in the seventh grade; then on to the required history course in eleventh grade. This is not as good as it sounds, for many schools will make a concerted effort to avoid repetition, so that students are given a once-over-lightly survey, beginning with the Indians and the colonial period in the fifth grade, continuing on to the Civil War in seventh, with a wrap up of whatever is left in the eleventh.

Lack of time is one reason for neglecting history, which has been identified in a study as only one of twenty-five subjects that come under social studies. History must compete with environmentalism, sexism, consumerism, social psychology, legal education, anthropology, and economics. Where a sense of purpose once reigned, confusion is now in the saddle. Education historian Diane Ravitch defines social studies thus: "To some teachers, social studies means the study of the social sciences, and many schools now offer courses in sociology, economics, psychology, and anthropology; to others it consists of studies that promote understanding of current social problems. Still others see it as a field whose purpose is to teach good behavior and good citizenship. A currently popular definition holds that its purpose is to teach values, critical thinking, and respect for cultural diversity." Chaos of this magnitude rarely develops overnight. Rather, social studies has been edging traditional subjects out of the curriculum ever since the National Education Association replaced its pro-academic stance with a social-adjustment philosophy in the early 1900s.

The vagueness of social studies today goes back to 1918 when the NEA published its "Cardinal Principles of Secondary Education," which were: (1) Health, (2) Command of Fundamental

Processes, (3) Worthy Home Membership, (4) Vocation, (5) Citizenship, (6) Worthy Use of Leisure, and (7) Ethical Character. "Citizenship demands that the social studies be given a prominent place," the NEA report states. But the NEA's idea of social adjustment as the way to good citizenship was a radical departure from the traditional view that the best foundation for citizenship is a study of this country's history and democratic institutions.

In 1926, eight years after the introduction of the "Cardinal Principles," the American Historical Association gave up its battle on behalf of history and joined with social scientists to form the Commission on the Social Studies in the Schools. "Thus, even the AHA had, in effect, conceded that school history was now one of the social studies, and that its role was to be viewed as 'useful' to citizenship training rather than as a liberal study," a 1985 AHA report concludes.

The quest for relevance, which accelerated in the 1960s, led to classes on contemporary issues and various forms of introspection. Subsequently social studies has been invaded by curricular fads promoted by special-interest groups and social-science experimenters. The consequent fragmentation of curriculum has produced a corresponding fragmentation in students' perception of the past. To quote Columbia Professor John A. Garraty, students "have no historical context" as a consequence of all the topics and themes courses they take.

The November 1967 *NEA Journal* heralded the change in the social studies as "a breaking away from the traditional dominance of history, geography, and civics. Materials from the behavioral sciences – economics, anthropology, sociology, social psychology and political science – are being incorporated into both elementary and secondary school programs." In the name of relevance students immerse themselves not in the causes of the fall of the Roman Empire, or in the ideas that inspired the Renaissance, or in the build up to and consequences of the

French Revolution, but in energy education, gun-control education, urban studies. You name it, social studies has got it – or can
order it for you.

Comparison shopping and anti-pollution campaigns may have
some relevance, but I suggest they are less relevant to a student's
education than knowing the causes of the American Revolution
or that the United States fought in World War II. But many high
school graduates have never heard of World War II, among
other things. Among the self-awareness components of social
studies, we have "values clarification." The teachers edition of
the Houghton Mifflin social studies series for kindergarten
through sixth grade discusses "strategies . . . designed to increase
empathy and decrease inclination toward egocentrism, ethnocen-
trism, and stereotyping." Among its many consultants is a "values consultant," a necessity since Houghton Mifflin promises to
improve children's "decision-making" and to contribute to their
"making valid judgments about problems facing our global
society."

The aspirations that curriculum designers have for students'
ability to draw conclusions about world problems are frequently
as high as the transmission of knowledge, via these textbooks, is
low.

Where history occurs in such curricula it remains on the
periphery as in Houghton Mifflin which promises "historical
materials [that] become a basic ingredient in the crucible of
learning, as children are motivated to introduce their own life
experiences and get involved in 'doing history.' " Let's look at the
fragments of history which are replacing an overall history.

Instead of the traditional survey course in history, we often
have the "mini-course" in such subjects as women's studies, black
studies, Hispanic studies. These mini-courses are not easily integrated into a chronological overview of history because students
lack the framework for this. Similarly, teachers, who may never
have taken a history course as part of the requirement for

becoming a social-studies teacher, are ill-equipped to place these fragments of history within their proper historical context.

Students on this restricted diet of minimal history, as prescribed by social scientists, forego one of the chief benefits of a knowledge of the past – a sense of perspective, the ability to differentiate between a crisis and a condition in a contemporary event. If perspective is what students miss, distortion is what they gain.

Mini-courses on black history, taught without a thorough grounding in the compromises and debates that led to the Civil War, and without a study of the subsequent Reconstruction period, distort, rather than illuminate, the history and current condition of race relations in this country.

The Council for Basic Education, in its report *Making History Come Alive*, criticized the fragmentation of human experience that results from mixing up the various social sciences – sociology with conditions of unemployment; political science with government; anthropology with comparative cultures. By contrast to social studies, the report claims, "history uniquely provides the continuity that gives human experience wholeness. And just as a tailor had better know all his customer's measurements before he cuts the sleeves and trousers of a suit, so a child in school needs to gain some comprehension of human experience whole before being able to make sense of the fragments." Let's consider examples of how history serves as handmaiden to social studies.

The "concepts-and-inquiry" approach to social studies is a prime example of how social science can distort reality to suit its purposes. For example, the American Revolution might be taught under a study of the concept of *loyalty*, which leads to a de-emphasis on a primary cause of the Revolution – taxation without representation. The concept of revolution itself might be treated under this approach, by having students leap from the

American Revolution, to the French, to the Russian, with a
pause to consider the revolution of the wheel.

Students thus presented with revolution as an abstraction,
rather than as a concrete event anchored in the many details of
its historic circumstances, may deduce similarities where they do
not exist. They will end such a course not seeing the American
War of Independence in all its unique complexity – which a
history study would point out – but as just one more in a series of
revolutions.

Much like concepts and inquiry, "global-studies" or "world-
studies" courses employ history as a means for explaining a
topic, rather than allowing history to stand on its own. In the late
1960s, the New York State Department of Education decided to
get trendy and adopted a history program which replaces the
chronological study of history with a basically present-oriented
study of topics and social-science concepts.

This study of the world focuses on ecology, human needs,
human rights, cultural interaction, the global system of economic
interdependence, and the future.

If students, for example, are studying the concept of economic
interdependence with a focus on Africa, they would examine
world business in Africa, resources needed for world trade, and
the effect of the continent's oil wealth on world politics. Within
this context, some aspect of the history of the African continent
would be taught. This is history on the periphery.

The attempt to crowd a range of concepts, issues and topics
into a course occurs also in the lower grades and is reflected in
textbooks too garbled for children to understand or teachers to
explain. One such textbook is *Cultures of the World*, for use in
the fourth grade, which compares cultures of Western Europe,
Java, Kenya, and Venezuela. The underlying message here is one
of cultural relativism, which works at cross purposes with the
idea that a school should transmit the basic ideas and history of
Western civilization.

In its comparison of four cultures, this book skips from environmentalism to government, from entertainment to shopping. Here the gesture toward history, in the section on Western Europe, consists of a mention of the dates of the Industrial Revolution. Consider the following paragraph: "The people of Western Europe went on inventing things. They also used inventions from other cultures. For example, Europeans learned about gunpowder, paper, printing and the magnetic compass. They put their knowledge to use. They invented guns. They invented printing presses. They learned how to build strong sailing ships. Then, with the help of the compass, Europe's sailors explored the world."

Notice the generalizations, typical of writers intent on giving a subject short shrift. This paragraph covers what history courses in an earlier era would have taught as the Age of Exploration and Discovery and the Renaissance. One can only lament the absence of what might have been: exciting stories on Ferdinand Magellan, Francis Drake, the Spanish Conquistadors, Queen Elizabeth I, the Spanish Armada.

When perusing deadly dull elementary school textbooks, replete with generalizations and abstractions of social science rather than the concrete details of history, one wonders if the social scientists kept their psychology consultants locked in the dungeon while they did their work upstairs. Children don't warm to abstractions but relish the specific and concrete, psychologists have told us for years. This incongruity further explains why children don't like social studies.

Even books labeled history, rather than world cultures or American studies, do not allow history to stand on its own merits, as writers strain to make analogies between recent events and those of the past. I discovered desperate attempts in several textbooks to associate Christopher Columbus' voyage to the New World with the U.S. space program. By thus bringing historic events up to date, these events are divorced from their historical context and are trivialized. In the gush of enthusiasm for the U.S. space program, the excitement and adventure of sailing the ocean in tiny ships with primitive instruments, in the face of pirates, mutiny and famine, as courageous men did four to five hundred years ago, is lost.

The most stunning aspect of relevance is that it has backfired on social scientists, as students frequently label social studies their most boring subject. The same students who doze under discussions of energy crisis and agricultural output or shopping in Venezuela might sit up and listen to the adventures of Marco Polo or to tales of the use of spies during the Civil War.

Ironically, even on an emotional level, history courses may prove to be more satisfying – translate relevant – than all the self-awareness courses offered under social studies. History has a liberating effect on the imagination that may help a child to solve his own problems. A child who reads a biography of Nathan Hale or Ethan Allen feels himself transported beyond himself, and a part of something bigger. Similarly, history frees the imagination of a child when he or she learns of an historic figure who survived difficult circumstances, as Abraham Lincoln did. Just as an immersion in current events imprisons us in the mundane crises of daily life, so can history provide a sense of release. A teacher, Martha Doerr Toppin, puts it this way: "A knowledge of the past increases our options. Things do not have to be the way they are in our neighborhood, in our suburb, in our time. We are not isolated in the present. We are not leashed to the limits of our own experience. We are not time's orphans."

History learned in school can provide emotional satisfaction long beyond the school years. It might even brighten the day of some of our policymakers. For, as historian Gilbert T. Sewall points out in an excellent book called *Against Mediocrity*, "The study of the achievements and ideals and policies of other times makes us less the slave of the present's supposed imperatives."

By imparting ability to judge worldly affairs, i.e., perspective, history can teach us more about the present than all the current-events courses that are replacing history in the schools today. Professor Jacques Barzun refers to this kind of judgment as "a permanent good, not because history repeats – we can never exactly match past and present situations – but because the tendency of things shows an amazing uniformity within any given civilization."

Unfortunately, students will not achieve the ability to make an informed judgment on events if the present approach of withholding history continues. Tragically, the anti-history trend not only threatens the well-being of these individuals, but the well-being of our whole society. NAEP survey results indicate that the decline in historical knowledge among students is accompanied by a declining ability to explain the essentials of democracy. This spells disaster for a country whose governing institutions depend upon the informed consent of the citizenry.

In his 1984 Jefferson Lecture, Professor Sidney Hook described a decline in faith in the essentials of democracy, a curious development because it coincides with progress toward ever greater freedom and social justice in this country over the past fifty years. Yet how are students to know, if they are not taught these facts?

Comparing American achievements with the wars, holocaust, economic misery, concentration camps and gulags of Nazi Germany and the Soviet Union, Hook pondered the paradox of declining faith in the principles of liberal democracy and noted, "Unless that faith and that belief can be restored and revivified, liberal democracy will perish."

Social scientists decry the teaching of the history of Western Civilization as "ethnocentric." Ironically, among the replacements for lessons about our heritage are narrowly focused ethnic-studies courses. But mini-courses which are indeed ethnocentric create small-minded voters, and the impact is already being felt in public life.

"We cannot be surprised at an electorate that refuses to rise above special-interest politics, if our schools teach only special-interest history," Professor Clair Keller notes in *Against Mediocrity*. "Students with no sense of the ways our *many histories* combine into the history of a single country cannot be expected to have sense of the public interest. For they have been taught that there are only *private* interests, and that one has common cause only with those whose private interests coincide with his own."

In summary, history has been subordinated to the study of social science within social studies. Social studies, from its inception a basically non-academic subject, is such a vague grab bag that it has become the vehicle for every issue that comes along. The social scientists unloaded their materials on social studies, the psychologists among them brought self-awareness and values clarification, and a host of special-interest groups have added ethnic-studies and current-issues courses. Add to this the cultural-relativism theories which work at cross purposes with the transmission of our own culture, and the chances for the survival of the history and ideas of Western civilization appear slim.

The antidote is not to discard social science and return to rote learning, heavy on dates, but rather to place history at the center of the curriculum with the various social sciences as illuminators of historic events. Throw out the textbooks and concentrate on the heroes and heroines of history, the carriers of the action.

Unless we restore history to its proper place, the consequences will be grave. By continuing to disregard history, we are cutting off a part of ourselves. From there we go to collective amnesia. If we forget on whose shoulders we stand, we will lose our footing. Once the memory of the past grows dim, we will forget who we are and why we exist as a people. Poised ready to relish the pleasure of the moment, without regard for how we became a free society, we risk losing all.

NOTES ON CONTRIBUTORS

Joseph Baldacchino is the author of *Economics and the Moral Order* and president of the National Humanities Institute. A *magna cum laude* graduate of Mount Saint Mary's College, he pursued graduate studies in political theory at The Catholic University of America. Among his scholarly essays are "The Value-Centered Historicism of Edmund Burke" and "Babbitt and the Question of Ideology." Baldacchino is associate editor of *Human Events*.

Solveig Eggerz is the author of *What's Wrong with the Public Schools?* and other works. Eggerz, who holds a Ph.D. in comparative literature from The Catholic University of America, was formerly on the faculty of that institution. She is working on a history curriculum for elementary schools.

Paul Gottfried is the editor of *The World and I*. A former chairman of the Department of History at Rockford College, Gottfried is editor of *Continuity: A Journal of History*. His books include *Conservative Millenarians, The Search for Historical Meaning* and *The Conservative Movement*, a book he coauthored with Thomas Fleming. Gottfried has been a Guggenheim Fellow.

Russell Kirk, a renowned lecturer, critic, and author of two dozen books, including *The Conservative Mind, Eliot and His Age, Enemies of the Permanent Things, The Roots of American Order,* and *Decadence and Renewal in the Higher Learning*, is chairman of the Academic Board of the National Humanities Institute. Kirk, who is perhaps the most influential American social thinker and man of letters of the last three decades, is the only American to have earned the highest arts degree of the senior Scottish university: doctor of letters of St. Andrews. Kirk has been a Guggenheim Fellow and a Senior Fellow of the American Council of Learned Societies.

Claes G. Ryn is professor and former chairman in the Department of Politics at The Catholic University of America. He has published several books, including *Will, Imagination and Reason, Democracy and the Ethical Life,* and *Nykonservatismen i USA.* Ryn has taught at Uppsala University (Sweden) and The University of Virginia. He is chairman of the National Humanities Institute.

Peter J. Stanlis, Distinguished Professor of Humanities Emeritus at Rockford College, is the author of *Edmund Burke and the Natural Law* and many other works, including studies of Robert Frost. He is also the editor of *Edmund Burke: Selected Writings and Speeches.* Stanlis is a member of the National Council on the Humanities and a member of the Academic Board of the National Humanities Institute.

INDEX

Abel, 41
Abolitionists, 54
Achilles, 40
*Advancement of Learning,
    The* (Bacon, F.), 75
Advertising, 21
Aeneas, 40
Aesop's Fables, 42, 72, 88
*After Virtue: A Study in Moral
    Theory* (MacIntyre), 40
*After Strange Gods: A Primer
    of Modern Heresy* (Eliot), 55
Against Mediocrity, 102, 104
Age of Exploration and Dis-
    covery, 101
Alaska, 94
Alienation, 76, 77
Allen, Ethan, 102
American Educator, The, 43-44
American Spectator, The, 51
American Civil Liberties Union,
    41
American Council of Learned
    Societies, 106
American Historical Associa-
    tion, 95, 97
"American Humanist" move-
    ment, 38
American Revolution, 98, 99,
    100
Anamnesis (Voegelin), 34n4
"Anatomie of the World, An"
    (Donne), 75-76
Andersen, Hans Christian, 42
Aristophanes, 35
Aristotle: and public education,
    52; 27, 37, 74, 77
Arnold, Matthew, 63, 65
Art: and universal ethical stan-
    dard, 30-31
Arthur, 40

Arthurian legends, the, 42
Augustine, St., 35

"Babbitt and the Question of
    Ideology" (Baldacchino), 105
Babbitt, Irving: and postwar
    American conservatives, 50;
    and neoconservatives, 51; and
    religion, 54-59; favored Chris-
    tian humanistic education, 56;
    his epistemology, 33n3; his in-
    fluence, 50; on imagination
    and reality, 17; on imagina-
    tion and will, 24; on purpose
    of literature, 38-39; on Wash-
    ington and Lincoln, 51-52, 57;
    on Woodrow Wilson, 52; on
    John Marshall, 57; on philan-
    thropy, 57-58; scolds Jeffer-
    sonian Democrats, 51; men-
    tioned, 35, 36, 39,, 46, 49, 61
Bach, Johann Sebastian, 32
Bacon, Francis, 66, 75
Bacon, Roger, 74
Baghdad, 94
Baldacchino, Joseph, 105
"Barn Burning, The" (Faulk-
    ner), 47
Barzun, Jacques, 103
Bauer, Gary: quoted, 42
Beatles, the, 32
Behaviorism, 37
Bennett, William J., 9, 41, 95
Bentham, Jeremy, 89
Benthamite utilitarianism, 89
Beowulf, 40, 72
Berkeley, George, 67
Bible, The, 40, 41, 59
Bierce, Ambrose: his definition
    of realism, 39